Muslims in India

The Growth and Influence of Islam

IN THE NATIONS OF ASIA AND CENTRAL ASIA

Afghanistan

Azerbaijan

Bangladesh

Indonesia

Islam in Asia: Facts and Figures

Islamism and Terrorist Groups in Asia

Kazakhstan

The Kurds

Kyrgyzstan

Malaysia

Muslims in China

Muslims in India

Muslims in Russia

Pakistan

Tajikistan

Turkmenistan

Uzbekistan

The Growth and Influence of Islam
IN THE NATIONS OF ASIA AND CENTRAL ASIA

Muslims in India

Mohammad Patel

Mason Crest Publishers
Philadelphia

Produced by OTTN Publishing, Stockton, New Jersey

Mason Crest Publishers
370 Reed Road
Broomall, PA 19008
www.masoncrest.com

First printing

1 3 5 7 9 8 6 4 2

Library of Congress Cataloging-in-Publication Data

Patel, Mohammad.
  Muslims in India / Mohammad Patel.
      p. cm. — (The growth and influence of Islam in the nations of Asia and Central
Asia)
  Includes bibliographical references and index.
  ISBN-13: 978-1-59084-881-4
  ISBN-10: 1-59084-881-0
  1. Muslims—India—History—Juvenile literature. I. Title. II. Series.
  DS432.M84P36 2006
  954.0088'297—dc22
                                              2005030439

Table of Contents

Introduction..7
   Harvey Sicherman, the Foreign Policy Research Institute

Overview 13

The Islamic Era 27

The Mughal Empire 41

The Establishment of the British Raj.....................53

The Path to Independence 69

Muslims in the Republic of India.........................93

Chronology 109

Glossary 111

Further Reading...112

Internet Resources..113

Index 114

Muslims pray at a mosque in New Delhi during Eid al-Adha (the Feast of Sacrifice), January 2006.

Dr. Harvey Sicherman, president and director of the Foreign Policy Research Institute, is the author of such books as *America the Vulnerable: Our Military Problems and How to Fix Them* (2002) and *Palestinian Autonomy, Self-Government and Peace* (1993).

Introduction

by Dr. Harvey Sicherman

America's triumph in the Cold War promised a new burst of peace and prosperity. Indeed, the decade between the demise of the Soviet Union and the destruction of September 11, 2001, proved deceptively hopeful. Today, of course, we are more fully aware—to our sorrow—of the dangers and troubles no longer just below the surface.

The Muslim identities of most of the terrorists at war with the United States have also provoked great interest in Islam as well as the role of religion in politics. It is crucial for Americans not to assume that Osama bin Laden's ideas are identical to those of most Muslims or, for that matter, that most Muslims are Arabs. A truly world religion, Islam claims hundreds of millions of adherents, from every ethnic group scattered across the globe. This book series covers the growth and influence of Muslims in Asia and Central Asia.

A glance at the map establishes the extraordinary coverage of our authors. Every climate and terrain may be found, along with every form of human society, from the nomadic groups of the Central Asian steppes to highly sophisticated cities such as Singapore, New Delhi, and Shanghai. The economies of the nations examined in this series are likewise highly diverse. In some, barter systems are still used; others incorporate modern stock markets. In some of the countries, large oil reserves hold out the prospect of prosperity. Other countries, such as India and China, have progressed by moving from a government-controlled to a more market-based economic system. Still other countries have built wealth on service and shipping.

Central Asia and Asia is a heavily armed and turbulent area. Three of its states (China, India, and Pakistan) are nuclear powers, and one (Kazakhstan) only recently rid itself of nuclear weapons. But it is also a place where the horse and mule remain indispensable instruments of war. All of the region's states have an extensive history of conflict, domestic and international, old and new. Afghanistan, for example, has known little but invasion and civil war over the past two decades.

Governments include dictatorships, democracies, and hybrids without a name; centralized and decentralized administrations; and older patterns of tribal and clan associations. The region is a veritable encyclopedia of political expression.

Although such variety defies easy generalities, it is still possible to make several observations. First, the geopolitics of Central Asia and Asia reflect the impact of empires and the struggles of post-imperial independence. Central Asia, a historic corridor for traders and soldiers, was the scene of Russian expansion well into Soviet times. While Kazakhstan's leaders participated in the historic meeting of December 25, 1991, that dissolved the Soviet Union, the rest of the region's newly independent republics hardly expected it. They have found it difficult to grapple with a sometimes tenuous independence, buffeted by a strong residual Russian influence, the absence of settled institutions, the temptation of newly valuable natural resources, and mixed populations lacking a solid national identity. The shards of the Soviet Union have often been sharp—witness the Russian war in Chechnya—and sometimes fatal for those ambitious to grasp them.

Moving further east, one encounters an older devolution, that of the half-century since the British Raj dissolved into India and Pakistan (the latter giving violent birth to Bangladesh in 1971). Only recently, partly under the impact of the war on terrorism, have these nuclear-armed neighbors and adversaries found it possible to renew attempts at reconciliation. Still further east, Malaysia shares a British experience, but Indonesia has been influenced by its Dutch heritage. Even China defines its own borders along the lines of the Qing empire (the last pre-republican dynasty) at its most expansionist (including Tibet and Taiwan). These imperial histories lie heavily upon the politics of the region.

A second aspect worth noting is the variety of economic experimentation afoot in the area. State-dominated economic strategies, still in the ascendant, are separating government from the actual running of commerce and industry. "Privatization," however, is frequently a byword for crony capitalism and corruption. Yet in dynamic economies such as that of China, as well as an increasingly productive India, hundreds of millions of people have dramatically improved both their standard of living and their hope for the future. All of them aspire to benefit from international trade. Competitive advantages, such as low-cost labor (in some cases trained in high technology) and valuable natural resources (oil, gas, and minerals), promise much. This is indeed a revolution of rising expectations, some of which are being satisfied.

Yet more than corruption threatens this progress. Population increase, even though moderating, still overwhelms educational and employment opportunities. Many countries are marked by extremes of wealth and poverty, especially between rural and urban areas. Dangerous jealousies threaten ethnic groups (such as anti-Chinese violence in Indonesia). Hopelessly overburdened public services portend turmoil. Public health, never adequate, is harmed further by environmental damage to critical resources (such as the Aral Sea). By and large, Central Asian and Asian countries are living well beyond their infrastructures.

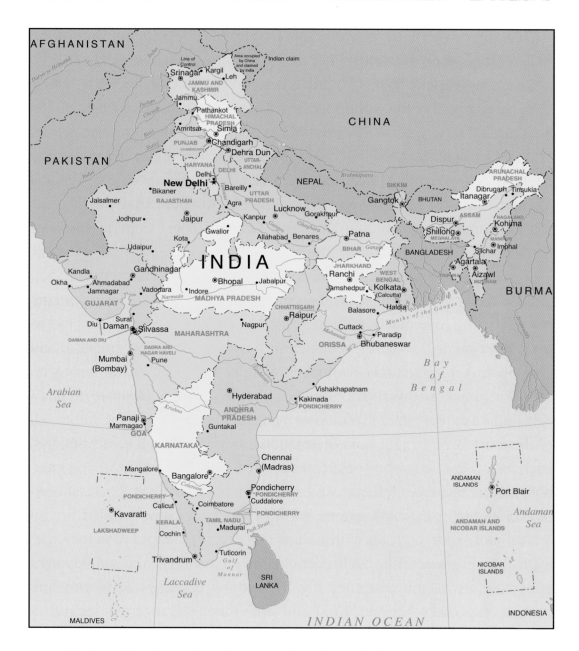

Third and finally, Islam has deeply affected the states and peoples of the region. Indonesia is the largest Muslim state in the world, and India hosts the second-largest Muslim population. Islam is not only the official religion of many states, it is the very reason for Pakistan's existence. But

Islamic practices and groups vary: the well-known Sunni and Shiite groups are joined by energetic Salafi (Wahabi) and Sufi movements. Over the last 20 years especially, South and Central Asia have become battle-grounds for competing Shiite (Iranian) and Wahabi (Saudi) doctrines, well financed from abroad and aggressively antagonistic toward non-Muslims and each other. Resistance to the Soviet invasion of Afghanistan brought these groups battle-tested warriors and organizers. The war on terrorism has exposed just how far-reaching and active the new advocates of holy war (jihad) can be. Indonesia, in particular, is the scene of rivalry between an older, tolerant Islam and the jihadists. But Pakistan also faces an Islamic identity crisis. And India, wracked by sectarian strife, must hold together its democratic framework despite Muslim and Hindu extremists. This newly significant struggle within Islam, superimposed on an older Muslim history, will shape political and economic destinies throughout the region and beyond. Hence, the focus of our series.

We hope that these books will enlighten both teacher and student about a critical subject in a critical area of the world. Central Asia and Asia would be important in their own right to Americans; arguably, after 9/11, they became vital to our national security. And the enduring impact of Islam is a crucial factor we must understand. We at the Foreign Policy Research Institute hope these books will illuminate both the facts and the prospects.

With more than 1 billion people, India is the world's second most populous country. This photograph shows a crowded bazaar in Mumbai, capital of Maharashtra state. The city, formerly known as Bombay, is home to more than 10 million.

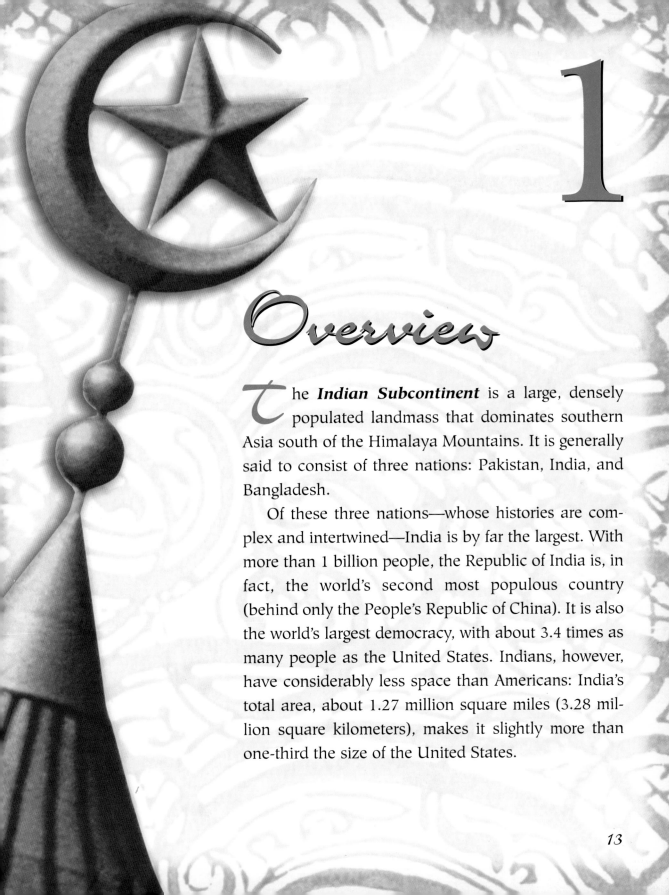

1

Overview

The **Indian Subcontinent** is a large, densely populated landmass that dominates southern Asia south of the Himalaya Mountains. It is generally said to consist of three nations: Pakistan, India, and Bangladesh.

Of these three nations—whose histories are complex and intertwined—India is by far the largest. With more than 1 billion people, the Republic of India is, in fact, the world's second most populous country (behind only the People's Republic of China). It is also the world's largest democracy, with about 3.4 times as many people as the United States. Indians, however, have considerably less space than Americans: India's total area, about 1.27 million square miles (3.28 million square kilometers), makes it slightly more than one-third the size of the United States.

A large crowd gathers along the sacred Ganges River, near its confluence with the Yamuna at Allahabad, 2001. The occasion is Maha Kumbh Mela, a six-week-long Hindu festival that takes place every 12 years and draws millions of Hindu pilgrims from all over India. By bathing in the Ganges during Maha Kumbh Mela, the faithful hope to purify themselves and release their soul from the cycle of birth and rebirth. About 8 in 10 Indians are followers of Hinduism.

Geography

India may be divided into three principal geographic regions. The Deccan Plateau, a large expanse of tableland, makes up the southern part of the country. Its northern boundary is conventionally fixed at the Narmada River, which runs east to west for about 800 miles (1,287 km) through the Indian state of Madhya Pradesh before emptying into the Gulf of Khambhat.

North of the Deccan lies the Indo-Gangetic Plain, a fertile region cut through by the Ganges River and its tributaries. The Ganges, considered sacred by many Indians, rises along the southern slopes of the Himalaya Mountains in India's Uttar Pradesh state. It flows south and then southeast through Uttar Pradesh, Bihar, and West Bengal before crossing into Bangladesh and merging with the Jamuna River. The Indo-Gangetic Plain is one of the world's most densely populated regions.

Northern India is dominated by the Himalaya mountain chain, which contains the world's tallest peaks. The Himalayas stretch in an arc from Jammu and Kashmir (ownership of which has long been a point of contention between India and Pakistan) eastward through Nepal, China, and

Bhutan and into Arunachal Pradesh, India's easternmost state. Northwestern India also contains a rugged mountain range, the Hindu Kush, which extends from western Kashmir into Pakistan and Afghanistan. Historically, the Himalayas and the Hindu Kush restricted the movement of peoples into the Indian Subcontinent.

Ethnic Diversity

The overwhelming majority of Indians come from one of two ethnic groups—Indo-Aryan (an estimated 72 percent of the population) and Dravidian (an estimated 25 percent). Linguistically and culturally, however, India is quite diverse. The national language, Hindi, is the primary tongue of only about 3 in 10 Indians. English, which has the status of associate official language, is the main language of national politics, commerce, and government. Fourteen other languages—Bengali, Telugu, Marathi, Tamil, Urdu, Gujarati, Malayalam, Kannada, Oriya, Punjabi, Assamese, Kashmiri, Sindhi, and Sanskrit—are also recognized as official, and some 800 dialects exist around the country.

India's rich and varied culture boasts a dazzling array of literary, artistic, and musical achievements. If indigenous peoples laid the foundations of Indian culture in ancient times, a succession of foreign settlers and invaders—including the Greeks, Persians, Portuguese, French, and British—later brought significant influences from outside the Subcontinent.

Throughout India's long history, religion has played an important role. Today, India is officially a secular country with no state religion. Yet more than 80 percent of Indians follow the Hindu faith, and Hinduism exerts a leading influence in Indian society.

Adherents of Islam, the second most widely practiced religion in India, make up only about 13 percent of the population. Yet because the country is so populous, that amounts to more than 135 million people—

A Hindu holy man meditates by the Ganges River.

enough to rank India as the second largest Muslim country, behind only Indonesia. Chronic tensions—punctuated by sporadic outbreaks of deadly violence—have marred Hindu-Muslim relations in parts of India (though it must be emphasized that peaceful coexistence is the rule throughout much of the country). In addition, there is a religious dimension to the often-antagonistic relationship between India and neighboring Pakistan, a Muslim nation.

Aside from Hinduism and Islam, a variety of faiths—including Christianity, Sikhism, Buddhism, Jainism, Judaism, and Zoroastrianism—are practiced in India. None, however, claims more than 2.5 percent of the population.

The Development of Indian Civilization

The Indian Subcontinent is home to one of the world's oldest civilizations. About 4,600 years ago, in and around the region of the Indus River valley (in present-day Pakistan and western India), cities and towns connected through a well-organized trade network and, probably, political alliances grew up where some of the earliest farming and herding communities had been established nearly two millennia before. Archaeologists have labeled the peoples who constructed, inhabited, and governed these urban centers the Indus Valley civilization or the Harappan culture (after Harappa, the town where evidence of the civilization was first uncovered).

The Indus Valley civilization extended across a huge area of at least 250,000 square miles (650,000 sq km), approximately the size of California and Wyoming combined. Its cities—which are carefully laid out with east-west and north-south boulevards and which frequently have extensive drainage systems for removing sewage—show a high degree of planning and organization. Archaeologists believe that, in addition to the widespread commerce within its territory, the Indus Valley civilization also traded with cultures in Mesopotamia (modern-day Iraq), the Persian Gulf, and Central Asia.

For some seven centuries, the urban centers of the Indus Valley civilization remained highly integrated and culturally cohesive. Sometime around 1900 B.C., however, this unification began to give way to regional fragmentation. Archaeologists today believe that the Indus Valley civilization did not disappear abruptly in the face of an invasion by outsiders, as had been postulated by earlier scholars. Rather, the once-unified culture is now thought to have evolved in distinct directions in different areas, surviving in some diluted (but still recognizably Harappan) form until perhaps 1300 to 1000 B.C.

The contention that the Indus Valley civilization was destroyed by outsiders fit into a larger theory on the origins of Vedic or Hindu culture. This theory—widely accepted for more than a century after its introduction in the mid-1800s but today mostly discredited—is referred to as the Aryan invasion theory. It said that, around 1500 B.C., lighter-skinned Indo-Europeans called Aryans swept into the Indian Subcontinent from the northwest, conquering the darker-skinned, indigenous Dravidians and introducing Hinduism.

Many contemporary scholars note the dearth of evidence to support this theory. Critics point out the racial and cultural bias implicit in the assertion that it took outsiders (with affinities to the European peoples) to plant the seeds of Vedic culture in India; they also claim that the Aryan invasion theory, which was first propounded by a German-born British scholar named Max Müller, conveniently served Great Britain's imperialist goals on the Subcontinent, in part by fostering divisions between India's Dravidians and Indo-Aryans, and in part by reinforcing the idea of European cultural superiority. In any case, there is much controversy today over how Vedic culture arose in India. Some scholars believe that, if they did not invade the Subcontinent, Indo-Aryan groups gradually migrated from Central Asia, and that these groups created Vedic culture. Others hold that Hinduism developed from the cultural exchange that took place when the migrating Indo-Aryans came into contact with Dravidian groups already residing in the Subcontinent. Still other specialists insist that Vedic culture evolved over many centuries entirely from within the Subcontinent (some even positing that Indo-Aryan groups actually originated in northwestern India and later migrated to Central Asia and Europe).

Hinduism

The term *Vedic* comes from the Vedas, sacred texts containing the essential truths of Hinduism. The Vedas—there are four collections—are compilations of poems and hymns in the ancient Sanskrit language. They were written down around the latter half of the second millennium B.C. but are believed to be based on older oral traditions.

The Rig-Veda, the longest, oldest, and most important of the Vedas, contains more than 1,000 hymns dedicated to a variety of gods. The other Vedas—the Sama-Veda, the Yajur-Veda, and the Atharva-Veda—include chants and invocations and detail the proper ways to perform various rituals.

Many Westerners have difficulty understanding Hinduism, and attempts to define precisely its tenets can be an exercise in frustration. This is due, in large measure, to the fact that Hinduism lacks a central creed, an organized religious hierarchy, or even a unified set of practices accepted by all believers. Rather, Hindus hold a broad range of beliefs and follow a variety of ritual practices. For the most part, Hindus do not seek converts; nor do they claim that theirs is the only path to spiritual truth. In fact, Hinduism has proved highly flexible in adapting to and assimilating a range of influences and ideas; it has thus evolved significantly over the centuries. And Hinduism is not simply a religion; it also represents a way of organizing society, influencing (if not dictating) an individual's social class and career options.

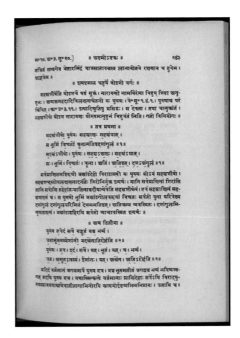

A page from the Rig-Veda. The oldest of Hinduism's sacred texts, it may have been composed in oral form before the fifth millennium B.C.

If exact, comprehensive definitions of Hinduism are elusive, some important generalizations can be made. First, Hinduism differs fundamentally from religions such as Judaism, Christianity, and Islam—which are all monotheistic faiths whose adherents believe in a personal God. In Hinduism many gods are worshiped, though all are manifestations of a single, supreme God known as Brahman. Yet it would be a mistake to equate "Brahman" with *God* in the sense that Westerners typically use the word; Brahman is more like an impersonal divine principle that permeates everything—the "oneness" of all that exists. That said, Hindus may—and many Hindus do—revere personal deities.

While Jews, Christians, and Muslims tend to see history in linear terms—with time inclining toward a future point at which God will judge humanity, rewarding the righteous and punishing the wicked—Hindus view time as cyclical. The universe is created, maintained, and then destroyed, only to be created anew in a never-ending cycle. The process takes place under the auspices of three gods or aspects of the divine principle: Brahma (the Creator), Vishnu (the Preserver), and Shiva (the Destroyer).

This conception of the cyclical nature of the universe finds a rough parallel in Hindu beliefs about the individual soul. Most Hindus (unlike their Jewish, Christian, and Muslim counterparts) believe in reincarnation, or transmigration of the soul into another body after death. *Karma*—essentially the consequences of one's actions in previous lives—determines the station to which one is born in a successive life. Bad deeds lead to rebirth into a less privileged social position (or even to rebirth as an animal); good actions lead to rebirth into a higher social position. The individual soul travels through many lifetimes as the cycle of birth, life (with all its accompanying misery), death, and rebirth is repeated (a cycle known as *samsara*). The ultimate goal, liberation or salvation from samsara, is called *moksha* or *mukti*. It marks the individual soul's union with Brahman (which may be described variously as the supreme universal soul,

This representation of Brahma, the creator god, is from a building in Tamil Nadu, India's southernmost state.

ultimate reality, or ultimate consciousness). Hindus believe that multiple paths can lead toward rebirth into a better life and ultimately to *moksha*, depending on the individual. These include meditation, scrupulous ethical and moral discipline, pursuit of right knowledge and right action, abandonment of attachment to the results of one's actions, elimination of passions, and devotion to a personal deity, particularly Rama or Krishna (incarnations of the god Vishnu).

A family of high-caste Brahmans, photographed during the late 19th century. Caste continues to play a major role in Indian society, influencing an individual's identity, status, and life prospects.

To the casual Western observer, one of the most striking—and objectionable—aspects of Hinduism is its seeming ordainment of social inequality. The **caste** system of hereditary social classes is central to Hindu beliefs and deeply ingrained in Indian society. Children are born into their father's caste, and throughout their lives they remain in that caste, which defines their social identity, status, and career choices and even influences whom they may marry and whom their friends may be. There are four main castes—Brahmans (composed of priests, scholars, and teachers), Ksatriyas (warriors, aristocrats, governors), Vaisyas (farmers, merchants, skilled laborers), and Sudras (servants or laborers). Within these four main castes are thousands of subcastes. Strict rules regulate behavior within and between castes. Breaking these rules can result in being shunned as an outcaste and not belonging to any community. Casteless "untouchables" (now called Dalits) were traditionally forbidden to have any contact with other members of society; it was even thought that touching the shadow of an untouchable would defile a member of a higher caste. In modern times India officially abolished "untouchability" and outlawed caste-based discrimination, but caste still influences everyday life.

Hindus believe that ethical and moral conduct, key to the individual soul's liberation, is determined by the principle of *varna-ashrama-dharma* (varna is caste, dharma is duty, and ashrama is one's stage of life). Righteous conduct lies in doing one's duty in accordance with one's caste and fulfilling the responsibilities associated with different periods of one's life (such as student, householder, or older person). The concept of *varna-ashrama-dharma* maintains order in Hindu society and legitimizes the status quo.

The Classical Period

Throughout history, Hinduism has proved highly flexible, adapting and assimilating beliefs from other religions. The middle part of the first millennium B.C. saw the founding of two major faiths that would present challenges to early Hinduism, which emphasized the importance of rituals and sacrifices and was dominated by the concerns of the Brahman priests.

Jainism, founded in northeast India in the sixth century B.C. by Mahavira ("the Great Hero"), rejected the caste system, the authority of the Vedas, and certain other Hindu beliefs and practices. Jains emphasize simplicity, good works, and consideration for all life as the path to the soul's liberation from the cycle of birth and rebirth, and they do nothing that may endanger an animal.

Buddhism also rejected the caste system, along with Hinduism's Vedic ritual. It was founded in the latter part of the sixth century B.C. by Siddhartha Gautama, known as the Buddha ("Enlightened One"). A wealthy prince from northern India who renounced the luxuries of palace life, he taught the "four noble truths": existence is sorrow; sorrow arises from earthly attachments; cessation of attachments ends suffering or sorrow; and nirvana (release from the cycle of birth and rebirth) can be achieved by following an "eightfold path" of spiritual discipline. Buddhism emphasized the importance of meditation and contemplation.

In the third century B.C., Buddhism was spread throughout much of India by Ashoka, a king of India's first imperial state, the Mauryan Empire. According to tradition, Ashoka—who ruled from around 273 to 232—was so repulsed by the carnage of a war he had successfully fought that he converted from Hinduism to Buddhism.

Hinduism adapted to the spread of Buddhism and Jainism by incorporating Buddhist and Jain practices and beliefs. Vedic rituals and sacrifices became less significant as meditation and contemplation assumed more importance. Many Hindus also adopted the values of nonviolence and concern for animals (including vegetarianism).

This renewed form of Hinduism had emerged by the start of the Gupta Empire (A.D. 320–550), which united northern India. From their capital Pataliputra (in the present-day Indian state of Bihar), the Gupta rulers presided over a golden age of Hindu culture. Important works of philosophy, poetry, drama, and Sanskrit grammar were written. Art and architecture flourished.

An invasion by Huns from Central Asia eroded the Guptas' power, however. By the early sixth century, their hold on northern India had been loosened, and the region soon fragmented into a host of smaller competing states. A king named Harsha, who came to power in 606, managed to reunite northern India under his strong rule. But at his death in 647, Harsha's kingdom disintegrated, and northern India again slipped into anarchy.

Muslim pilgrims pray before the Kaaba in Mecca, Saudi Arabia. Before the triumph of the prophet Muhammad and his followers in A.D. 630, this ancient shrine—which Muslims believe was constructed by the patriarch Abraham and his son Ishmael and which they consider the holiest place on earth—contained pagan idols.

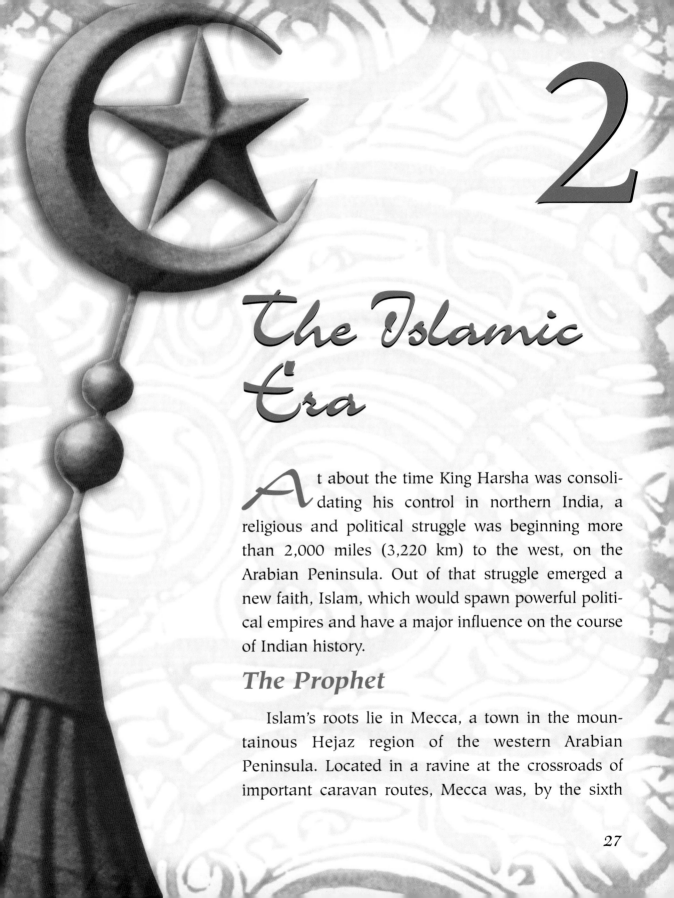

2

The Islamic Era

At about the time King Harsha was consolidating his control in northern India, a religious and political struggle was beginning more than 2,000 miles (3,220 km) to the west, on the Arabian Peninsula. Out of that struggle emerged a new faith, Islam, which would spawn powerful political empires and have a major influence on the course of Indian history.

The Prophet

Islam's roots lie in Mecca, a town in the mountainous Hejaz region of the western Arabian Peninsula. Located in a ravine at the crossroads of important caravan routes, Mecca was, by the sixth century A.D., a prosperous trading center. It was also an important destination for religious pilgrims, who flocked to Mecca to worship the many idols housed in a cube-like shrine known as the Kaaba. Arabs at this time were polytheistic; they worshiped several hundred gods and goddesses.

Islam's founder, Muhammad, was born in Mecca around 570. His tribe, the Quraysh, effectively functioned as Mecca's ruling class; the tribe controlled the Kaaba shrine and included the town's leading merchants. Muhammad's father died before the boy's birth; six years later, when his mother died, Muhammad became an orphan. He was raised by an uncle, Abu Talib.

Muhammad tended sheep and worked as a camel driver during his youth. He gained a reputation for honesty and trustworthiness, qualities that attracted the attention of a wealthy Meccan widow named Khadija, for whom Muhammad worked as a caravan agent. In 595, when Muhammad was about 25 years old and Khadija 40, they married.

Muhammad settled into the life of a merchant, but he was distressed at the idolatrous religious practices of his fellow Arabs and at the way wealthy Meccans treated the poor. Over the years, he retreated periodically to a cave on nearby Mount Hira in order to contemplate. Muslims believe that there, around 610, Muhammad received the first of what would be a lifelong series of revelations from Allah (the Arabic word for "God"), conveyed by the angel Gabriel. These revelations would later be transcribed as the Qur'an (also spelled Koran), Islam's holy scripture.

Initially, Muhammad shared his revelations only with Khadija and a small group of close friends and relatives. By 612, however, he had begun preaching Allah's message more openly. This led to conflict with Mecca's Quraysh leaders and merchants, for what Muhammad had to say directly threatened their privileged status.

Islam fundamentally challenged the status quo in Mecca first because of its monotheism. Muhammad said that there is but one God, and that everyone must submit to His will (the word *Islam* comes from an Arabic term meaning "submission" or "surrender"). In polytheistic Mecca, this proposition contradicted people's basic religious beliefs. But it also had significant economic implications: if pagan idols were not to be worshiped, the Quraysh stood to lose the considerable money they made from pilgrims to the Kaaba. Furthermore, Muhammad preached that the rich had an obligation to treat the poor with respect—and must even share some of their wealth with the less fortunate.

As more people—particularly among the lower classes—were attracted to Muhammad's message and became Muslims ("those who

A page from the Qur'an, Islam's sacred scripture. Muslims believe the Qur'an contains the actual words of Allah (God) as revealed to the prophet Muhammad.

surrender" to God), Mecca's leaders took steps to contain Islam. They passed laws forbidding all social and business relations between Muslims and non-Muslims. This caused great hardship for the Muslims, some of whom were unable to earn a living and starved to death. More violent forms of persecution followed. Muslims were beaten and sometimes even murdered. A plot was hatched to kill Muhammad.

Finally, in 622, Muhammad and his followers fled to the town of Yathrib, located about 210 miles (338 km) north of Mecca. This event, known as the *Hijra*, is conventionally said to mark the beginning of the Islamic era.

(Above) This painting depicts the *Hijra*, the exodus of Muhammad's followers from Mecca in A.D. 622. The embattled group settled in the oasis town of Yathrib, north of Mecca. **(Right)** After the *Hijra*, Muhammad and his followers established—and successfully defended—the first Islamic society. Yathrib was renamed Madinat al-Nabi ("City of the Prophet"); today it is better known to English-speakers as Medina. This photo shows Medina's Prophet's Mosque, whose initial construction dates to the year 622.

In Yathrib, Muhammad and his followers established the first Muslim community and built the first mosque. The town was soon renamed Madinat al-Nabi ("City of the Prophet"). Today it is known in English as Medina.

Tensions between the Muslims and the Meccans persisted even though the two groups were now separated by hundreds of miles of desert.

Warfare erupted in 624 when Muhammad led a 300-man force against a Meccan caravan in what became known as the Battle of Badr. Though the Meccans enjoyed a three-to-one numerical advantage, the Muslims triumphed. Over the next few years, the fighting continued intermittently. As more Arab tribes converted to Islam, the advantage swung to the Muslim forces. In 630, defeated and dispirited, Mecca surrendered to Muhammad, and most of the town converted voluntarily to Islam.

The Spread of Islam

At the time of Muhammad's death in 632, Islam had spread across the Arabian Peninsula. Within a century a vast Islamic empire had been established. In the west, it streched across North Africa and into Europe's Iberian Peninsula (present-day Spain and Portugal); in the east it encompassed what is today called the Middle East and reached into Central Asia.

The remarkable expansion of Islam in such a relatively short period can be explained by several factors. First, Muslim armies were fierce, well organized, and highly motivated. They won much territory for Islam by the sword. Second, for many people the tenets of Islam held considerable appeal. Islam's values are egalitarian and its rituals relatively simple and straightforward; Islam emphasizes the believer's direct relationship with God rather than requiring the performance of esoteric rituals or the intercession of a specialized clergy. Anyone can become a Muslim by making a simple profession of faith, called the *shahada* ("There is no God but Allah, and Muhammad is His Messenger"), and following a few basic duties of believers. In addition to the *shahada*, the fundamental obligations of the faithful, or Five Pillars of Islam, are *salat*, prayers performed five times daily; *zakat*, the giving of a portion of one's wealth to charity; *sawm*, fasting between dawn and dusk during the holy month of Ramadan; and *hajj*, a ritual pilgrimage to Mecca, which all believers who are able must undertake at least once in their lifetime. As the Islamic empire expanded, many

A Muslim in Srinagar, the summer capital of Jammu and Kashmir, bows toward Mecca in prayer. He is among the more than 135 million Indians who follow the Islamic faith.

people who came under its rule willingly converted because of Islam's spiritual appeal. For pagan peoples, however, the choice was frequently between conversion and death (even though the Qur'an forbids forced conversion). While Jewish and Christian subjects were generally not compelled to convert, they did have to pay a special tax, known as the *jizya*, and were considered *dhimmi*, protected (if in many ways second-class) citizens. Economic considerations thus spurred some Christians and Jews to become Muslims.

Islam on the Indian Subcontinent

Islam is believed to have first reached the Indian Subcontinent around the middle of the seventh century, with seafaring Arabs who traded in the region of Sind, in present-day southern Pakistan. In 711, ostensibly in response to the piracy of an Arab vessel, the Muslim governor of Iraq launched an invasion of Sind. The Arab forces crossed Baluchistan (in present-day western Pakistan), swept into the Indus Valley, and overwhelmed the area's Hindu *rajas*, or rulers. Initially, Hindus who refused to convert were killed; later they were granted *dhimmi* status.

For more than two centuries Islamic control on the Indian Subcontinent was largely limited to Sind. In the late 10th century, however, Muslim armies crossed the rugged mountains of Afghanistan and thrust into north-western India, inaugurating a period of raiding and, eventually, conquest and consolidation that brought the Punjab region under Muslim control.

The first raid from Afghanistan was conducted in 986 by Subuktigin, the Turk ruler of Ghazni and founder of the Ghaznevid dynasty. After Subuktigin's death in 997, his son Mahmud of Ghazni continued these incursions into India. Beginning around 1000, Mahmud (971–1030) launched as many as 17 raids, ultimately taking his armies across northern India to the banks of the Ganges River.

Mahmud seems to have been motivated in part by a desire to spread Islam through jihad, or "holy war." Known as "the Idol Smasher," he destroyed Hindu idols, artwork, and temples; he also massacred large numbers of "infidel" Hindus. But plunder was probably at least an equally important motive. Mahmud looted gold and jewels and carried thousands of women and slaves back to Ghazni. Among the important Hindu cities Mahmud sacked were Somnath (in the present-day Indian state of Gujarat) and Mathura and Kannauj (both in Uttar Pradesh). By 1026 Mahmud had annexed the Punjab into his empire.

Muslim chroniclers wrote many accounts of Mahmud's exploits. A number of these writers demonstrate little or no first-hand knowledge of India, and there is good reason to suspect that some of the stories they include are not entirely accurate. Nevertheless, a vivid picture emerges of great destruction, suffering, and carnage inflicted upon Hindus by the Muslims. For example, in the account written by Utbi, Mahmud's personal secretary, the sultan is said to have taken 500,000 slaves after defeating the Hindu king Jaipal in 1001. Mahmud destroyed 10,000 temples, Utbi reports, after taking Kannauj in 1019. And when Mahmud sacked Somnath about five years later, Utbi says that more than 50,000 Hindus

in all manners and usages, [the Hindus] differ from us to such a degree as to frighten their children with us, with our dress, and our ways and customs, and as to declare us to be devil's breed, and our doings as the very opposite of all that is good and proper. By the bye, we must confess, in order to be just, that a similar depreciation of foreigners not only prevails among us and the Hindus, but is common to all nations towards each other.

The small kingdoms of northwestern and northern India, while they shared the Hindu religion, were too fragmented to present a unified defense against the Muslim invaders. These kingdoms were ruled by members of a Hindu warrior caste known as the **Rajputs**, who were deeply divided by clan loyalties. Although Mahmud raided at will, he did not pay much attention to consolidating his rule in the territories he plundered. After he died, his empire disintegrated, and the Muslims lost control of the Punjab.

The Delhi Sultanate

Around the middle of the 12th century, a Persian Islamic dynasty known as the Ghurids took control of Ghazni in Afghanistan. In 1173 the Ghurid prince Muhammad of Ghur was made the sultan of Ghazni. Two years later he invaded northern India, and within two decades Muhammad had conquered as far as Delhi. Returning to Afghanistan, Muhammad left his most trusted general, a Turkic slave named Qutb-ud-din-Aybak, in charge of the conquered territory in India.

After Muhammad was assassinated in 1206, Qutb proclaimed himself the first sultan of Delhi. Over the succeeding centuries the Delhi Sultanate, India's first Muslim kingdom, would see five major dynasties: the Slave (or Mamluk) dynasty (1206–1290), the Khalji dynasty (1290–1320), the Tughlaq dynasty (1320–1413), the Sayyid dynasty (1414–1451), and the Lodi dynasty (1451–1526). The Delhi Sultanate's power waxed and waned, and relations with Hindus varied, during the reigns of different sultans.

The first sultan, Qutb-ud-din-Aybak, died in a fall from his polo pony in 1210. He was succeeded by his son-in-law, Shams-ud-din Iltemish (Iltutmish), who guaranteed Hindus *dhimmi* status and allowed Hindu chiefs who paid revenues to control their territories. Shams-ud-din Iltemish's daughter Raziyya became the only Muslim woman to rule on Indian land.

The Khalji dynasty sultan Ala-ud-Din, who ruled from 1295 to 1315, brought large new territories in the southern part of India under Muslim control. Ala-ud-Din treated his Hindu subjects rather harshly, imposing high *jizya* taxes on them and compelling peasants to sell their grain only to his licensed dealers.

Muhammad ibn Tughlaq (ruled 1325–1351), founder of the Tughlaq dynasty, was more sympathetic to Hindus; he even appointed a Hindu **amir** (the highest official except for the sultan). But Ibn Tughlaq's personal eccentricities and his pursuit of some unpopular and ill-advised policies spurred a series of rebellions, and territories in southern India that Ala-ud-Din had won began to break away. These included the Hindu Vijayanagar kingdom, founded in 1336; it would grow into a powerful empire and stand as a bulwark against Muslim intrusion in southern India for two centuries. Also lost to the Delhi Sultanate during Ibn Tughlaq's reign was the Muslim Bahmani kingdom, established in 1347 by Bengal's rebellious military governor; it eventually broke into five South Indian states ruled by Turks and Indian Muslims (this cultural blend influenced Hyderabad, which remained a **princely state** until 1948).

The last strong Delhi sultan was the Tughlaq dynasty's Firuz Shah (ruled 1351–1388). An orthodox Muslim, he is credited, according to historian Stanley Wolpert, with the construction of 40 mosques, along with 30 colleges, 100 hospitals, 50 dams and reservoirs, and 200 new towns. He was also hostile to Hindus. Visiting a village where a Hindu fair was being held, Firuz ordered the fair's organizers put to death. He had a

Ruins of the Hindu kingdom of Vijayanagar, which broke away from the Delhi Sultanate in 1336 and stood in the way of Muslim expansion into southern India for more than two centuries.

Brahman burned alive for worshiping in public. He demolished many Hindu temples and replaced them with mosques.

Though it lingered for more than 135 years after Firuz Shah's death, the Delhi Sultanate was reduced to little more than a local power by the

Turkish conqueror Timur Lenk (better known to Westerners as Tamerlane). The grandson of the feared Mongol leader Genghis Khan, Timur (1336–1405) sacked Delhi in 1398. His armies killed countless Hindus and took some 100,000 slaves before Timur left India in 1399 after reaching Meerut.

The Sayyid dynasty, whose rulers came from the family of Timur's viceroy, claimed power in Delhi in 1414. But their power did not extend much beyond the city of Delhi itself, and by 1451 they had been overthrown by the Afghan Lodis.

The splendor of Mughal rule in India is epitomized by the Taj Mahal. Built by the 17th-century Mughal emperor Shah Jahan in memory of his beloved wife Mumtaz Mahal, the mausoleum blends Muslim, Hindu, and Persian influences.

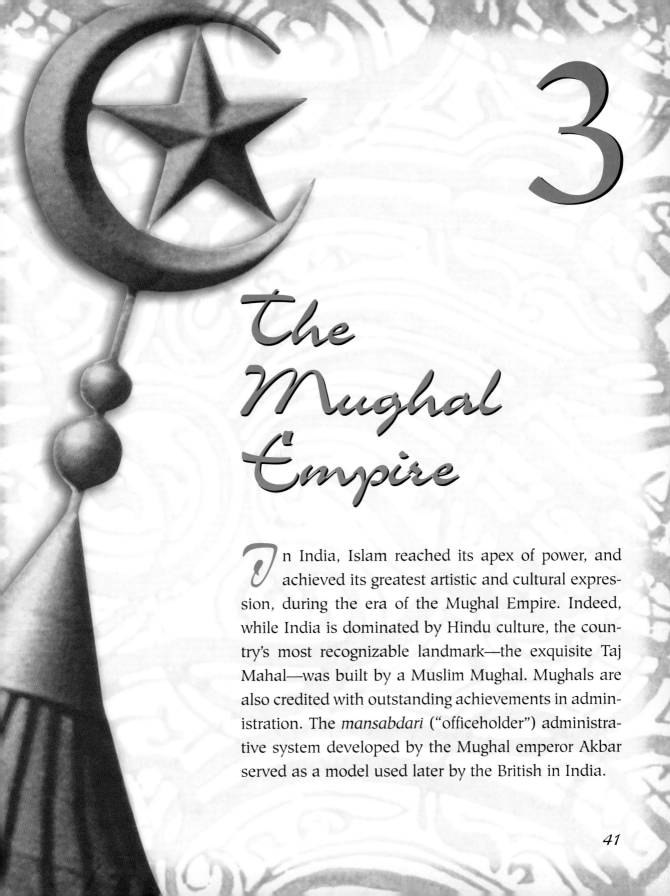

3

The Mughal Empire

In India, Islam reached its apex of power, and achieved its greatest artistic and cultural expression, during the era of the Mughal Empire. Indeed, while India is dominated by Hindu culture, the country's most recognizable landmark—the exquisite Taj Mahal—was built by a Muslim Mughal. Mughals are also credited with outstanding achievements in administration. The *mansabdari* ("officeholder") administrative system developed by the Mughal emperor Akbar served as a model used later by the British in India.

The term *Mughal* (or *Mogul*) is believed to be a language corruption of *Mongol*, which means brave or bold. The Mongols were a pastoral people who, under the leadership of Genghis Khan, swept out of their homeland in Mongolia during the 13th century and conquered huge territories in Asia and Europe. The founder of the Mughal Empire, Babur, was a descendant of Genghis Khan and the great-grandson of Timur Lenk.

The Founding of the Mughal Empire

Originally named Zahir-ud-din Muhammad, Babur (1483–1530) was a prince of the Persian Timurid dynasty. Upon his father's death in 1495, he became king of Fergana (in present-day Uzbekistan); two years later he expanded his realm by conquering Samarkand (also in Uzbekistan). The young king suffered a setback in 1501, losing Fergana and Samarkand. He then marched to Kabul, which he captured in 1504.

After trying unsuccessfully to regain Samarkand, Babur turned his gaze eastward toward the Punjab. He conducted a series of raids between 1519 and 1524. In 1525 he led an army of about 12,000 horsemen across the Indus River. On April 26, 1526, about 50 miles (80 km) north of Delhi, Babur met the army of Ibrahim Lodi, the last Delhi sultan. With 100,000 soldiers and 1,000 war elephants, Ibrahim's forces greatly outnumbered those of Babur. But Babur was a bold, capable tactician, and he used mobile artillery and quick-moving cavalry to rout Ibrahim

Babur, the founder of the Mughal dynasty, was a descendant of the feared conquerors Genghis Khan and Timur Lenk.

at the First Battle of Panipat. The following year Babur defeated the powerful ruler Rana Sanga's Rajputs at the Battle of Khandwa in present-day Madhya Pradesh. In 1529 he won an important victory over the ruler of Bengal and allied Afghan chiefs.

Known for his strength, courage, and military ability, Babur also had a great love for nature and the arts. He established famous gardens in Kabul, Lahore, and Agra, and his memoirs, *Babur-Nama*, detailed Mughal garden design. The hard-fighting Mughals appreciated elaborate gardens within palaces and forts as places to relax, hold ceremonies, and even be buried. Their designs, inspired by the Qur'an to represent paradise on earth, combined dramatic sites, water features, planting, and architecture. They cultivated flowers such as violets, jasmine, and roses alongside trees and shrubs for color and shade and even grew produce such as grapes and melons.

Babur died in 1530 and was succeeded by his son Humayun (1507–1556). Humayun immediately faced a dispute with his brother, to whom he ceded Kabul and the western part of Punjab. From there his rule became even shakier. Within a decade the Afghan king of Bengal, Sher Khan (also known as Sher Shah), had unseated Humayun, who found refuge at the court of Persia's Safavid dynasty in Tabriz.

With help from the shah of Persia, Humayun regained power in Kabul during the mid-1540s. In 1555 he returned to India and conquered Delhi. The newly reinstalled Mughal ruler brought with him master artists from Tabriz, who established the first Mughal book painting studio, which blended Persian and Indian styles. But Humayun ruled only a few months before he fell down a staircase and died.

Akbar the Great

Humayun's son and heir, Jalal-ud-din Muhammad, better known as Akbar the Great (1542–1605), was only 13 years old at his father's death

Akbar the Great— a bold general, brilliant administrator, and tolerant ruler—greatly expanded the Mughal Empire. His 50-year reign was marked by excellent relations between Hindus and Muslims and by myriad cultural achievements.

in 1556. Until Akbar came of age, his longtime guard Bayram Khan would help him rule, serving as both chief minister and general. Bayram and Akbar wasted little time in consolidating and expanding the Mughal realm. In 1556 they won an important military victory at the Second Battle of Panipat. Five years later, now ruling on his own, Akbar began a successful, decade-long campaign to conquer the Rajput princes. In 1566 he invaded Punjab. He conquered Gujarat in 1572–1573, Bengal in 1576, and Kashmir in 1586–1592. In 1592 he annexed the Sind. His empire now extended across almost all of northern India.

If Akbar was a great general, he was also a brilliant administrator. Open-minded and tolerant, he surrounded himself with capable people, whether Hindu or Muslim. He made allies of Rajput chiefs. A Hindu noble, Bhagwan Das, became one of his chief generals. Raja Todar Mal, his Hindu adviser, army commander, and revenue minister, helped compose uniform laws and revenue collection and assessment reforms based on Indian custom. In his *mansabdari* system, he appointed 33 ranks of officials called *mansabdars*, who were paid salaries instead of being rewarded with land grants, as had been the practice. The select higher ranks included a significant number of Hindus.

Akbar's reign was marked by excellent relations between Hindus and Muslims. Unlike other Mughal rulers, Akbar never attempted to abolish Hindu practices and customs. In fact, he promoted cultural accommodation and assimilation in his empire. In 1562 he married the daughter of a

Hindu raja, and he encouraged intermarriage between the Mughal and Rajput nobilities. In 1564 he abolished the *jizya* taxes that non-Muslims had been forced to pay. He ceased enslaving prisoners of war and outlawed forced conversions to Islam.

Akbar turned away from the orthodox practice of Islam and embraced Sufism, the religion's mystical tradition. Eventually he incorporated ideas from other faiths to found, in 1580, the *Din-i-Ilahi* ("Divine Faith") as a unified religion for his empire. But it gained few followers and outraged orthodox Muslim leaders.

Over a 15-year period Akbar constructed a magnificent new capital for his empire, Fatehpur Sikri. Located 23 miles (37 km) west of Akbar's old capital, Agra, Fatehpur Sikri was built atop a ridge overlooking a small village. Its buildings and monuments—including a red sandstone palace,

A view of Fatehpur Sikri, Akbar's magnificent but short-lived capital. The site was abandoned after a scant 15 years, possibly because of a contaminated water supply.

monuments, courtyards, halls of justice, council chambers, and tombs—fused traditional Hindu and Islamic elements into an Indo-Muslim architecture. For example, Fatehpur Sikri's structures featured Islamic domes but had Hindu square windows and doorways in place of Persian arches. By 1585, however, Fatehpur had to be abandoned, possibly because the artificial lake supplying its water was polluted.

Akbar's reign produced other impressive cultural achievements. A patron of the arts, Akbar supported Hindu and Muslim writers, poets, musicians, and artists (including more than 100 painters working at his court). His protégé Tulsi Das wrote inspirational poetry based on Indian myth and the life of the Hindu god Rama.

Intrigue and Opulence

Akbar's long and splendid reign came to an untimely end on October 17, 1605, after he was poisoned by his son, the half-Rajput Jahangir. Like the father he murdered, Jahangir loved poetry and painting and was a patron of the arts. Unlike Akbar, however, he was also overly fond of such pleasures as wine and beautiful women. Throughout much of his reign, while Jahangir was distracted by the pursuit of these pleasures, his beautiful Persian wife, Nur Jahan, wielded a great deal of power. Nur Jahan (whose name means "Light of the World") attracted large numbers of Persian artists, poets, and scholars to the Mughal court. But she also appointed many of her own family members to official positions, and they acquired a reputation for corruption. Discontent among Mughals simmered.

For his part Jahangir managed to destroy much of the intercommunity harmony that his father had so assiduously cultivated. He promoted mass conversion to Islam, persecuted Jains, and alienated Sikhs.

By the early 1620s Nur Jahan's influence in the court, particularly her attempts to maneuver a favorite prince into a position to succeed

Jahangir, provoked rebellion by one of Jahangir's younger sons, Prince Khurram (1592–1666). At Jahangir's death, on October 29, 1627, Khurram—who had earlier been placed in command of the army—moved decisively. He immediately executed relatives who were rivals to the throne and exiled Nur Jahan to Lahore.

Upon ascending to the Mughal throne, Khurram took the name Shah Jahan, which means "King of the World." He seemed determined to live up to that grandiose title during a reign that lasted almost 40 years. Shah Jahan commissioned a throne studded with huge diamonds, rubies, sapphires, emeralds, and pearls; it became known as the "Peacock Throne." His harem numbered some 5,000 women. Shah Jahan created ornate gardens at Shahjahanabad and Lahore. But the opulence of his reign is most evident in the

Attendants serve the Mughal emperor Jahangir and his favorite wife, Nur Jahan, in this 17th-century miniature painting. Jahangir, who was greatly attached to the pleasures of court life, allowed the beautiful and ambitious Nur Jahan to accumulate vast influence—often to the detriment of his empire.

buildings he constructed, especially the Jama Masjid and the Taj Mahal.

The Jama Masjid—built in Delhi from 1644 to 1658 and dedicated to Shah Jahan's favorite daughter, Jahanara—is India's largest mosque. Its central courtyard, covering more than 100,000 square feet (9,920 square

After winning the fight to succeed Jahangir, Khurram (above) took the name Shah Jahan ("King of the World"). During almost 40 years of rule, he spent extravagantly, maintaining a court that was opulent even by Mughal standards and constructing magnificent gardens and buildings, including the Taj Mahal and India's largest mosque, the Jama Masjid (opposite page).

meters), accommodates 25,000 worshipers. The red sandstone and white marble mosque features a pattern of swirling and interlocking designs known as arabesques. Its twin minarets (towers from which a Muslim official known as the muezzin calls the faithful to prayer) rise 130 feet (40 meters).

Some 20,000 workers—including skilled architects, inlay craftsmen, calligraphers, stone carvers, and masons—worked for more than 17 years, from 1631 to 1648, to build the structure for which Shah Jahan is best known: the Taj Mahal. Situated along the banks of the Yamuna River in Agra, the Taj Mahal is a mausoleum for Shah Jahan's favorite wife, Mumtaz Mahal, who died in childbirth. Its architecture—lavish yet balanced and well proportioned—blends Muslim, Hindu, and Persian influences. The brokenhearted emperor spared no expense in the monument to his beloved wife: the Taj Mahal's white marble is inlaid with semi-precious stones (some small inlaid lotus flowers contain as many as 350 gemstones such as amethyst, jade, carnelian, onyx, jasper, coral, and turquoise). It seems to change color with the changing light and is said to glow in the moonlight. The mausoleum houses the graves of the emperor, his wives, and other Mughal royalty. There is also a mosque inside. Pathways, channels, and rows of fountains bisect the garden's square lawns.

Shah Jahan expanded the Mughal Empire by conquering part of the Deccan (though he also suffered defeat in Afghanistan). But while he spent lavishly on his court and his many building projects, administration

of the empire suffered. For example, Shah Jahan's government contributed a meager weekly amount in relief for starving peasants during a horrible famine.

Shah Jahan, like his predecessors, was a patron of the arts. Hindu and Mughal artists in his court developed a distinctive painting style. He also allowed Europeans to establish settlements in Mughal lands.

In 1658 the ailing Shah Jahan was deposed by his son Aurangzeb (1618–1707), who wished to seize the initiative in a fight with his brothers over succession. For the remaining eight years of his life, Shah Jahan remained a prisoner in the famous Red Fort of Agra.

Decline and Fall

After seizing the Mughal throne in 1658, Aurangzeb killed his three brothers, consolidating his power. He took the name Alamgir ("World Conqueror").

Over the next five decades, Aurangzeb fought a series of wars to expand his empire. He waged a long, costly, and ultimately inconclusive campaign against the Marathas, a new Hindu power around the area of Poona (now Pune) to the west. Under the leadership of Sivaji (1627–1680), the Marathas waged an effective guerrilla fight, ambushing the slow-moving Mughal armies, encumbered by their heavy equipment and long supply lines. In the 1660s, Sivaji gained control of Mughal territory by capturing strategic Mughal forts.

Aurangzeb achieved better results in the Deccan. There, after years of fighting, he managed to conquer the Muslim kingdoms of Bijapur and Golkonda.

Despite this territorial expansion, the Mughal Empire was collapsing from within. Corruption was rampant. Unrest among peasants and uprisings by local rulers, combined with Aurangzeb's far-flung military expeditions, sapped the army's strength.

A devout Sunni Muslim who wanted to restore Orthodox Islam, Aurangzeb constantly alienated his Hindu subjects. In 1668 he outlawed Hindu religious fairs and banned the building of new temples and the repairing of old ones. He ordered the destruction of some old temples. He later imposed a special tax on Hindu males old enough to bear arms, revived the Hindu poll tax, and doubled the duty imposed on Hindu merchants. Protesters were crushed to death by the emperor's war elephants.

In 1675 Aurangzeb's soldiers arrested and beheaded Tegh Bahadur (1621–1675), the ninth Sikh guru, for refusing to convert to Islam. The Sikhs subsequently became a military order. To protect Sikhs against persecution, the 10th guru, Gobind Singh (1666–1708), created the Khalsa ("Pure Ones") sect of warriors, men and women recruited mainly among peasants in the Punjab. A powerful Sikh empire would later be established in the Punjab.

Aurangzeb, who ruled from 1658 to 1707, is considered the last powerful Mughal emperor.

In 1681 Aurangzeb's son Akbar, joined by Hindu kingdoms in Rajasthan, rose up against his father. Although the rebellion was later joined by the Maratha king Raja Sambhaji (Shivaji's son), Aurangzeb eventually managed to suppress it.

Aurangzeb died in 1707. Although the Mughal Empire would endure in some form for an additional 150 years, it would never regain its past glory. Rebellions by local rulers and wars with foreign powers steadily diminished the Mughal realm and led to the creation of many small independent states in northern India.

Akbar the Great receives Sir John Mildenhall, ambassador of Queen Elizabeth, 1599. Mildenhall's mission, which he successfully discharged, was to apply for trade privileges within the Mughal Empire on behalf of the soon-to-be-chartered British East India Company. From these small beginnings, the British would ultimately gain control over the entire Indian Subcontinent.

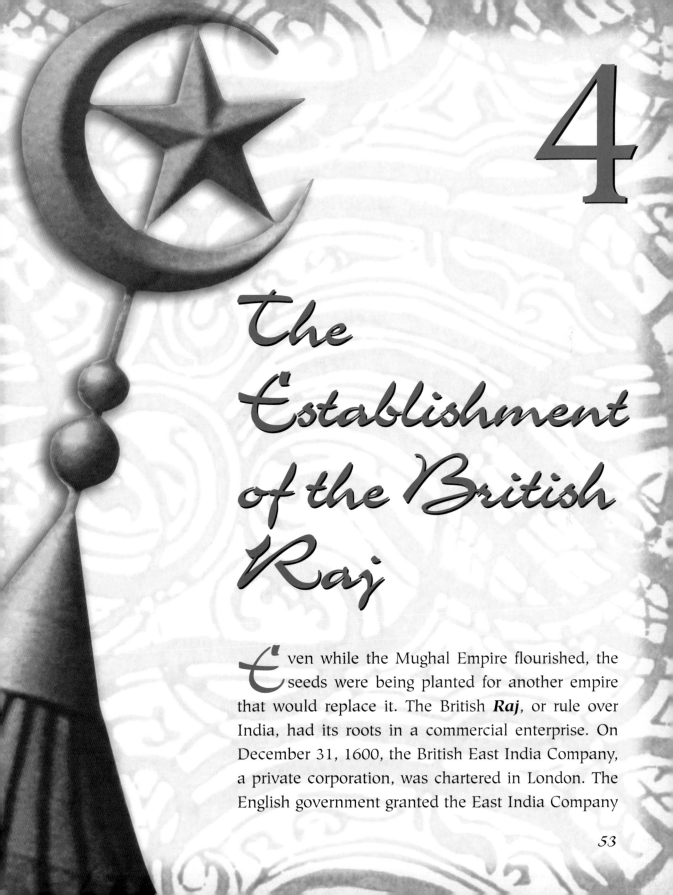

4

The Establishment of the British Raj

*E*ven while the Mughal Empire flourished, the seeds were being planted for another empire that would replace it. The British *Raj*, or rule over India, had its roots in a commercial enterprise. On December 31, 1600, the British East India Company, a private corporation, was chartered in London. The English government granted the East India Company monopoly rights on all British trade with India and the Far East. Before the end of the 17th century, the East India Company had firmly established itself on the Subcontinent, acquiring trading rights in Madras (1639), Bombay (1664), and Calcutta (1696).

In many respects India proved an ideal place for the British merchants to do business. Europe craved goods from the East, including silk, china, calico, and tea, and labor in India was cheap—one pence a day versus six back in Britain—so the goods were inexpensive to produce. By 1744 the East India Company had enough money to loan the British government 1 million pounds, a sum equivalent to $230 million today.

British and French Rivalry

England wasn't the only European country involved in the Far East trade, however. Over the years, Portugal, France, the Netherlands, and Denmark had competed for the lucrative trade—and the latter three had also chartered private East India companies. By the mid-1700s, the French Compagnie des Indes Orientales, established in 1664, had emerged as a major rival of the British East India Company. In 1744, when European politics drew their respective nations into war, the two companies—which maintained private armies—began fighting each other in India.

Local Indian rulers bristled at the sight of foreigners waging war on their soil. In Karnataka, located in southern India, the Mughal **nawab** Anwar-ud-Din sent an army of 10,000 men to attack a force of 230 Frenchmen and 700 hired Indian soldiers, or **sepoys**. The French forces fired a musket volley and then led a bayonet charge. In a pattern that would be repeated often, the native army was unprepared for European-style warfare. Anwar-ud-Din's forces fled in disarray.

Military superiority was crucial in enabling the Europeans to extend their influence in India. This typically did not involve the direct conquest of local populations, however. Rather, the East India companies strategically backed one local ruler against another—in exchange for commercial concessions. (There were many opportunities, as India at the time had some 650 separate princely kingdoms.) For instance, in return for its assistance in helping him regain his throne, the deposed raja Shahaji agreed to pay tribute to and give the British East India Company the port of Tanjore (Thanjavur). This process would repeat itself many times, as the company traded protection for money and influence.

In the south, the French gained control by putting their chosen rulers in power. After the death, in 1748, of Nizam-ul-Mulk, the ruler of the Deccan region, the Compagnie des Indes threw its support behind Muzafar Jang as his successor. With this aid, Muzafar was able to defeat two rivals and assume the throne. He rewarded his patrons with large territorial grants. When Muzafar was assassinated, the French placed Saladat Jang in power. In Karnataka, Anwar-ud-Din was killed and replaced by Chandra Singh, and gifts to the Compagnie des Indes flowed in. France now effectively held much of southern India.

The East India Company was not willing to let that situation stand. Karnataka, in particular, was seen as an essential thoroughfare for trade. Robert Clive, who had arrived in India in 1744 as a clerk for the East India Company and had risen to battlefield command, made the daring decision to attack Karnataka's capital at Arcot.

By the time Clive's forces arrived, the garrison in Arcot had fled, leaving the city undefended. But soon after the East India Company's army moved in, it was trapped within the city walls by Chandra Singh's French-backed forces. The French siege lasted 50 days, until Morari Rao, a chief of Maratha, arrived with his cavalry. Unbeknownst to the French, Clive had forged an alliance with Rao, and together they were able to rout Chandra's forces. Arcot marked a turning point in the war between the East India Company and the Compagnie des Indes. The English under Clive began winning victories and collecting Indian allies.

By the time he posed for this portrait, painted around 1755, Robert Clive had enjoyed a meteoric rise from clerk for the British East India Company to military hero. His crowning achievement, however, was still two years in the future.

As the East India Company collected allies, its officers collected riches. In exchange for placing a nawab in charge of his princely kingdom, Robert Clive accepted lavish gifts and the company accepted yearly tribute. This, combined with ever broadening trade, made the East India Company the richest and most powerful force in the region.

The Coup in Bengal

At the same time it was battling the Compagnie des Indes in the south, the East India Company began increasing its influence in Bengal. The most populous region in India, Bengal was thought to contain more than 40 million people (though there was no official census). In the early 1740s the Muslim governor of Bengal, Ali Vardi Khan, broke away from the declining Mughal Empire and established his own bustling kingdom. The East India Company had secured trading rights that exempted it from paying levies, which deprived the nawab of revenue and was an affront to his sovereignty. But the British were not about to give up the concessions they had been granted. Tensions simmered.

In the summer of 1756 Ali Vardi Khan's son and successor, Siraj-ud Daula, finally moved against the East India Company's fort in Calcutta. Ill equipped and undermanned, the garrison was quickly overwhelmed. What followed was an incident that would come to be remembered notoriously as "the Black Hole of Calcutta." According to British accounts—which, it must be emphasized, many Indian scholars consider wildly exaggerated if not entirely fabricated—the nawab confined 146 captured British soldiers in a small, closed room, and half suffocated.

The episode outraged the British. Clive retook Calcutta and signed a truce of convenience with Siraj, who now needed British support to stave off invading Afghans from the northwest. Meanwhile, Clive began plotting Siraj's downfall. He promised money to Hindu and Sikh enemies of the nawab and secured the cooperation of Mir Jafar, Siraj's general, whom he promised to install as the new nawab.

On June 23, 1757, Clive's East India Company army met the forces of Siraj-ud Daula at the Battle of Plassey. As arranged, Mir Jafar turned on Siraj, and many of the soldiers in the nawab's army—who had been bribed

His hat raised, Robert Clive pays respects to Mir Jafar, the newly installed nawab of Bengal. Mir Jafar's betrayal of the previous nawab, Siraj-ud Daula, helped ensure Clive's victory at the Battle of Plassey on June 23, 1757. Plassey, in turn, paved the way for the British Raj.

not to fight—deserted. Not surprisingly, the Muslim forces that did fight were soon routed, and Siraj was chased down and killed.

While not a significant military engagement, the Battle of Plassey is conventionally cited as the beginning of the British Raj. Mir Jafar gave locally collected taxes to the East India Company (and, later, to Robert Clive personally). The East India Company, which previously had been involved only in export trade, soon controlled Bengal's internal trade markets.

When Mir Jafar, recognizing that he had no actual power, decided to take control of his state, the British simply deposed him and appointed a new nawab, Mir Kasim. For his part, Mir Kasim also wanted to control Bengal. He went about replenishing the coffers and retreated to a remote city, where he began building and training a modern army with European mercenary artillerymen. Joined by Shuja-ud Daula, the nawab of Awadh, and by the Mughal emperor Shah Alam II, Kasim met the British at Buxar in 1764. Again, however, the British routed the Indian forces. With Kasim's defeat, the East India Company's hold on Bengal was truly secure. The Mughal emperor ceded all right to tax collection to the East India Company. And in the south, company forces triumphed decisively over the French.

The British East India Company now controlled a large part of the Subcontinent. Company officials had not planned to conquer India; they were simply businessmen who had taken the most expedient route to profitability—for the company as a whole and, increasingly, for themselves as individuals. Whether through bribery, duplicity, or sheer ruthlessness, they removed all who stood in the way of their accumulation of wealth.

Concerns in England

India had become very important to England in the century and a half since the British East India Company received its royal charter.

Shah Alam II delivers a decree ceding to the British East India Company all rights to tax collection in his realm. The armies of the Mughal emperor and his allies had earlier been crushed at the 1764 Battle of Buxar.

India generated a huge volume of trade and commerce for Britain; in addition, the East India Company owed the British government a direct annual payment of £400,000 to maintain its monopoly rights. But British government oversight of the administration of India had always been minimal. Given the distance between India and England and the slowness of communications at the time—it took up to nine months from the dispatch of a message to the receipt of a response—East India Company officers could not reasonably be expected to defer all important decisions until first consulting London. But many officials in the British government were deeply troubled by the East India Company's methods and believed, with justification, that the organization was rife with corruption and operated largely above British law.

By the early 1770s, after tea sales to the restive American colonies plunged, the East India Company was unable to make its £400,000 annual payment to the British government. In 1773, when the company's royal charter came up for renewal, Parliament took the opportunity to pass the Regulating Act. Although the East India Company retained overall control in India, the act reorganized the company's structure, limited its authority, and gave the British government greater oversight powers. Among its provisions, the Regulating Act established the post of governor-general of Bengal and created a Governing Council, whose members were appointed by the Crown; created a supreme court in Calcutta that had royal judges and claimed jurisdiction over all British subjects, as well as their Indian servants, in Bengal; and, in an effort to stamp out rampant corruption, prohibited all officials from accepting any gift or reward from any Indian.

Only a decade after the Regulating Act went into effect, the British government took further measures to assert the Crown's authority in India. Under the India Act of 1784, the East India Company retained the power to fill positions in India (subject to the king's veto) and still made all trade decisions. But a six-member Board of Control, headed by England's chief finance minister and with members drawn from British government circles, was put in charge of overseeing diplomatic, administrative, and revenue matters and could issue orders that the East India Company's officers were obliged to carry out.

The dual structure of British authority in India—with trade falling under the purview of the East India Company and the Crown taking more responsibility for governance—lasted into the middle of the 19th century. During this period, the armies of the East India Company expanded British control on the Subcontinent. By 1818 the Hindu Maratha states of central India had been conquered. In 1843 the British defeated the

Muslim amirs of the Sind. And after two bloody wars, in 1845–1846 and 1848–1849, the East India Company annexed the wealthy Sikh kingdom of Punjab.

Governing the vast Subcontinent, however, was complicated by cultural differences between the British rulers and their Indian subjects. Before about 1830, British officials in India generally took a pragmatic approach, allowing Indians to retain many of their customs and traditions, even if those practices offended British sensibilities. As English governors in India, spurred in part by Christian missionaries, sought to compel Indians to abandon their traditions, tensions mounted. Hindus, for example, were offended when, in 1827, the British outlawed sati (or suttee). In this traditional practice, a wife would voluntarily immolate herself on her deceased husband's funeral pyre as an expression of devotion. Laws passed in 1850 secured property rights for Hindus who converted to Christianity and guaranteed Hindu widows the right to remarry. Both measures were affronts to Hindu culture, adding to the sense that traditional life was in peril.

Princes also resented the East India Company policy banning the longstanding practice by which Hindu rulers adopted sons in order to ensure succession. Under what was called the "doctrine of lapse," the East India Company annexed the realms of princes who died without fathering a male heir.

The Indian Rebellion

Suspicion and resentment of the British, among Hindus as well as Muslims, exploded in 1857 in the Indian Rebellion. Because the rebels were sepoys—the Indian professional soldiers employed by the East India Company—the rebellion was widely known as the Sepoy Mutiny.

In early 1857 rumors spread that the greased-paper cartridges used in the new Enfield rifles the sepoys had been issued were lubricated with cow and pig fat. This offended Hindus and Muslims equally, as cows are sacred in the Hindu faith and Muslims consider pigs unclean. The outrage of the sepoys was compounded by the fact that, in loading a rifle round, the soldier tore the paper cartridge with his teeth. Thus Hindus might be defiled by consuming part of a cow, and Muslims by consuming part of a pig.

In February a native regiment refused to use the ammunition in question, prompting the British to stop using animal fat to lubricate rifle cartridges. But sepoys continued to suspect the British of attempting to subvert their religion. On March 29, on a parade ground near Calcutta, a sepoy named Mangal Pande exhorted his comrades in the 34th Bengal Regiment to rise up, and he shot a British officer. While widespread carnage was averted that day, the British were alarmed—and with good reason: the sepoys greatly outnumbered their English officers throughout India.

The British responded by disbanding any regiment—including the 34th Bengal—whose loyalties seemed questionable. This did nothing to defuse the situation, as it left many men without work and without pensions.

The first large uprising broke out in the city of Meerut, after an English commander, Colonel Carmichael Smyth, arrested sepoys who refused his order to load their carbines with greased-cartridge ammunition. On May 10, comrades of the arrested sepoys broke them out of jail, gathered a mob of discontented civilians, and murdered any English people they could find, including women and children.

The violence quickly spread to Delhi, where the Indian regiments joined the uprising and British officers abandoned the city. The mutineers called for a restoration of the Muslim Mughal dynasty and rallied around the aging Bahadur Shah. The last Mughal emperor in India, Bahadur had been given the title king of Delhi, though he lived on a British pension and under British supervision.

This engraving, originally published in 1867 in the *Illustrated London News*, depicts violence in Meerut during the Indian Rebellion. The bloody uprising among Indian professional soldiers employed by the British—known at the time as the Sepoy Mutiny—broke out in Meerut in May 1857 and then spread to other areas of British India.

The East India Company's response to the uprising was hampered by lack of manpower. Most of the white troops were in small groups between Delhi and Calcutta. Only 3,800 troops were available to lay siege to rebel-controlled Delhi. Forces from across Asia and Africa were diverted to India, but their arrival would take weeks or months.

Meanwhile, the revolt spread. In Cawnpore the mutineers gained support from Nana Sahib, a local prince whose claim to a British pension had been rejected. Nana slaughtered the entire British garrison of the city, including 125 women and children who were murdered on the night of July 15. Such atrocities were by no means confined to the rebels, however.

British soldiers forced Muslim prisoners to eat pork and Hindu prisoners to eat beef before proceeding to hang them.

While the mutiny shook British control, the rebels lacked unified leadership and failed to seize the initiative when numbers were most to their advantage. Rebel sepoys remained holed up in Delhi, for example, rather than braving artillery fire in an attempt to scatter the outnumbered British troops laying siege to the city. The sepoys' failure to act decisively gave British reinforcements time to gather. In August, as the desertion of rebel sepoys reduced their numbers inside the city gates to between 30,000 and 40,000, the British managed to assemble a force of 46,400 white and 58,000 loyal Indian soldiers. On September 14, the British forces stormed Delhi, which was captured after six days of bloody fighting. Bahadur Shah was found and exiled. Mutineers who escaped fled southeast to the city of Lucknow, which subsequently fell on March 15, 1858. The British then pushed eastward and defeated Nana Sahib's forces.

Rebuilding the Raj

In the wake of the Indian Rebellion, the British government rethought its administrative policies on the Subcontinent. It abolished the East India Company and transferred direct authority in India to the British Crown (though it would be nearly 20 years before Queen Victoria formally took the title Empress of India). The English monarch was given the power to appoint a viceroy of India, who ruled from Calcutta. With the approval of the English monarch, the viceroy appointed lieutenant governors to administer the various British possessions. The British cabinet post of secretary of state for India was also created.

On November 1, 1858, the new government of India was announced. Rebels who surrendered before the new year would be pardoned, provided they had not participated in massacres. The British also abandoned the doctrine of lapse, announced that treaties with former princely states would be honored, and returned land that had been seized.

In the succeeding years, the British undertook a variety of infrastructure projects, including railroads, bridges, and irrigation works. Administrative and educational reforms were also instituted, particularly under Lord Curzon, who served as viceroy from 1899 to 1905. British knightly orders were reinstated and bestowed liberally on local princes and soldiers, and princes frequently visited England, where they were treated to extravagant welcomes. All of these measures can be seen as attempts to create goodwill among Indian petty princes and commoners. The ultimate goal was to make India—considered the jewel of the British Empire—more profitable and easier to govern.

Lord Curzon, who served as viceroy of India from 1899 to 1905, instituted a series of educational and administrative reforms.

Yet the British efforts to placate their Indian subjects met with only mixed success. In 1883, for example, a proposal to permit Indian judges to hear cases against Europeans—widely supported by native Indians—was quashed by the vehement protests of whites in India. Continuation of the practice of trying Europeans in India only before white judges led many Indians to conclude that the justice system was stacked against them. Famines struck India in 1895–1896 and 1899–1900, and British relief efforts were perceived as somewhat callous, as victims had to travel

Starving Indians in Ahmadabad wait to receive food rations, ca. 1900. The British practice of making famine victims travel to work camps in order to receive food assistance cost lives that otherwise might have been saved and alienated many Indians.

to work camps in order to receive food assistance. Many died as a result. Even British efforts to extend education to Indians caused resentments. In the first place, only a minority of Indians ever received a British education; most Indians continued to be illiterate. Secondly, the elite few who did obtain a university education were often frustrated by limited job prospects, as native Indians were generally excluded from high-status fields such as the law and medicine, and civil service positions in the Raj administration were mostly reserved for the English-born. As a nationalist movement in India sprouted, these educated, disenfranchised Indians would play crucial roles.

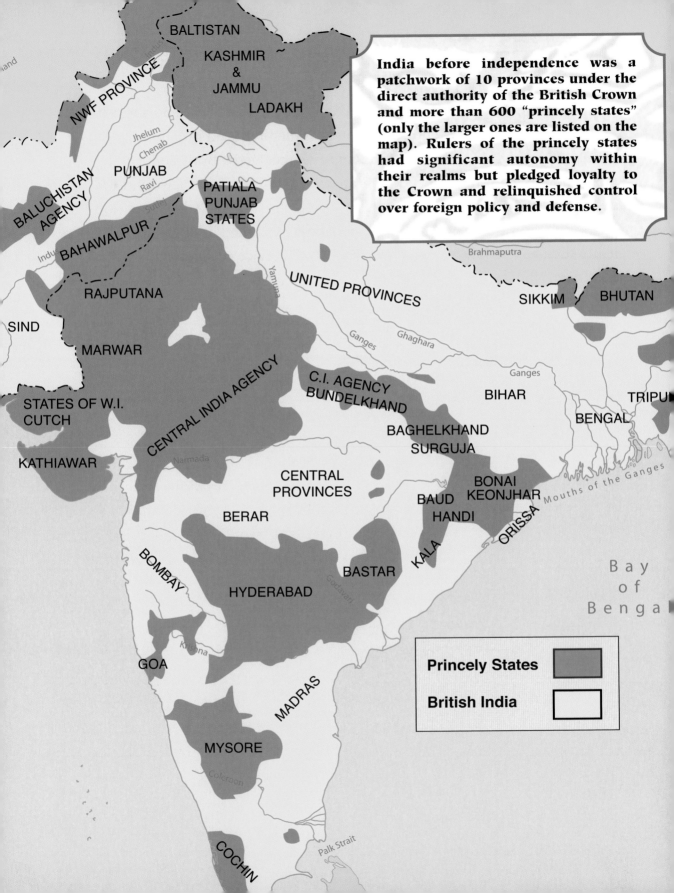

India before independence was a patchwork of 10 provinces under the direct authority of the British Crown and more than 600 "princely states" (only the larger ones are listed on the map). Rulers of the princely states had significant autonomy within their realms but pledged loyalty to the Crown and relinquished control over foreign policy and defense.

BALTISTAN

KASHMIR & JAMMU

LADAKH

NWF PROVINCE

Jhelum

Chenab

BALUCHISTAN AGENCY

PUNJAB

Ravi

PATIALA PUNJAB STATES

Sutlej

Indus

BAHAWALPUR

RAJPUTANA

Yamuna

UNITED PROVINCES

Brahmaputra

SIKKIM

BHUTAN

SIND

MARWAR

Ganges

Ghaghara

Ganges

STATES OF W.I. CUTCH

CENTRAL INDIA AGENCY

C.I. AGENCY BUNDELKHAND

BIHAR

TRIPU

BENGAL

BAGHELKHAND

SURGUJA

KATHIAWAR

Narmada

CENTRAL PROVINCES

BONAI KEONJHAR

Mouths of the Ganges

BAUD HANDI

BERAR

BOMBAY

HYDERABAD

BASTAR

KALA

ORISSA

Bay of Bengal

Godavari

GOA

Krishna

MADRAS

Princely States

British India

MYSORE

Coleroon

Palk Strait

COCHIN

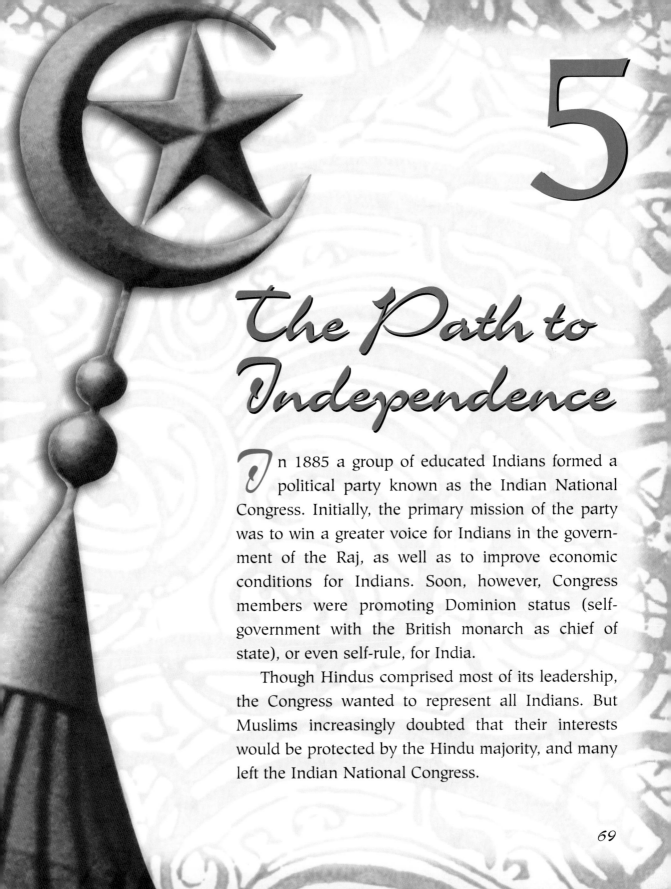

5

The Path to Independence

*I*n 1885 a group of educated Indians formed a political party known as the Indian National Congress. Initially, the primary mission of the party was to win a greater voice for Indians in the government of the Raj, as well as to improve economic conditions for Indians. Soon, however, Congress members were promoting Dominion status (self-government with the British monarch as chief of state), or even self-rule, for India.

Though Hindus comprised most of its leadership, the Congress wanted to represent all Indians. But Muslims increasingly doubted that their interests would be protected by the Hindu majority, and many left the Indian National Congress.

By the turn of the 20th century, simmering Hindu-Muslim tensions were occasionally boiling over into localized violence. Some conflicts centered on issues such as the Muslim killing of cows or Hindu defiling of mosques. Other resentments were more deep-seated. As the British gradually opened up the civil service and high-status professions to Indians, it was mostly Hindus who received the jobs. In 1905, in an effort to contain intercommunity violence, the British partitioned Bengal into predominantly Hindu West Bengal and predominantly Muslim East Bengal. The move won wide support from Muslims, who believed it would open up political and economic opportunities for them. But wealthy and prominent Hindus were outraged, sensing that their political and economic status was threatened. To protest the partition of Bengal, Hindus organized a boycott of British goods, which further angered Muslim traders and spawned more unrest. By 1911 the British, recognizing that the partition had failed, reunited Bengal.

But the incident galvanized Muslims to organize politically in order to protect their interests. In 1906 the All-India Muslim League, which would become a formidable rival of the Indian National Congress, was founded.

The Raj confronted further unrest in 1907, after the lieutenant governor of the Punjab instituted a new tax on farmers and **zamindars** who relied on government waterworks to irrigate their land. Vociferous protests came from landowners as well as the normally quiet peasantry. But most disturbingly to the Raj, there were rumors of unrest among Punjab-born soldiers, who constituted more than a quarter of the Indian army. Unwilling to risk another mutiny, the government repealed the new tax.

Against the backdrop of this and other unrest, the British took a step toward Indian self-rule with the passage of the Government of India Act of 1909, popularly known as the Morley-Minto Reforms. Most significantly, the reforms provided for a limited number of Indians to be elected to an executive council to the viceroy and to legislative councils for the provinces. While the number of Indians who were eligible to vote was small, and the viceroy and provincial governors did not have to heed the direction of the councils, the idea of direct elections had been introduced, and Indians had an official legislative forum in which to express their opposition to the Raj.

The Effects of World War I

During the First World War (1914–1918), the Indian army fought with Britain and the Allies (principally France, Russia, and the United States) against the Central Powers (Germany, Austria-Hungary, and the Ottoman Empire). Many Indian nationalists believed that by supporting the British Empire in its time of need, India could expect to be rewarded with greater self-rule after the war was over. In addition, the right of self-government was a major principle enunciated by the victorious Allies, which seemed to bode well for the Indian nationalist cause.

While Britain did not grant India self-government, it did undertake further reforms aimed, according to the British government, at "increasing association of Indians in every branch of the administration and the gradual development of self-governing institutions with a view to the progressive realization of responsible government in India as an integral part of the British Empire." The Government of India Act of 1919, also known as the Montagu-Chelmsford Reforms, increased the number of eligible voters and gave the legislative councils more responsibility. Ultimately Britain planned to allow Indians to control the law-making process at home while Britain retained authority over foreign policy.

The Rise of Gandhi

The Montagu-Chelmsford Reforms failed to satisfy everyone, and opposition to British policies continued. The pan-Islamic Khalifat Movement focused Muslim dissatisfaction with the British and caused

some six minutes later. According to the official account, 379 people were killed and 1,200 wounded, but the actual numbers may have been considerably higher.

After the massacre, Dyer carried out floggings and other humiliations in order to impress upon Punjab residents that the Raj was still in control. Among the British, it was generally accepted that a successful revolt in Punjab would lead to a widespread revolt even more serious than the 1857 Sepoy Mutiny.

While some in England hailed Dyer as a hero for saving the Raj, he was eventually removed from active command and encouraged to retire. In India the Jallianwala Bagh massacre provoked outrage and spurred Gandhi in 1920 to initiate a campaign of noncooperation with the British.

Gandhi's plan, which was embraced by the Indian National Congress, would make India impossible for the British to govern without resorting to violence. And this, Gandhi believed, would prick the collective conscience of the British, who would see that the only moral course was to grant India self-government. As he would later explain, his purpose was to convert the British, not to harm them. Indians taking part in the noncooperation campaign would give back their titles and decorations, not attend official ceremonies, keep their children from going to school, boycott the courts, refuse to pay taxes, refuse to purchase imported goods, and refuse to participate in elections. Eventually, the Congress asked all Indians working for the government to resign.

Again, however, the essential principle of nonviolence was largely lost. Riots broke out across India. Many people saw the campaign as an opportunity for retribution for past wrongs, undermining Gandhi's entire philosophy.

In February 1922, with his prediction that the Raj would give way still unfulfilled, Gandhi suspended the noncooperation campaign, concluding that many of his fellow Indians were not ready for the demands of nonviolent resistance. The following month he was arrested for sedition. He pled guilty, declaring, "I do not ask for mercy. I do not plead any extenuating act. I am here, therefore, to invite and cheerfully submit to the highest penalty that can be inflicted upon me for what in law is a deliberate crime and what appears to me to be the highest duty of a citizen." Gandhi was sentenced to six years' imprisonment, though he was released in 1924 for medical reasons. Over the next several years, he largely stepped out of the public eye, retiring to a simple life of prayer, fasting, and cotton spinning, which he had promoted as a symbol of Indian economic self-sufficiency.

Self-Rule Moves Forward

To a certain extent, Gandhi's vision had unified Hindu and Muslim nationalists. With his departure from public life, however, divisions

Gandhi reads correspondence after his release from prison, May 1924. His first satyagraha campaign having ended in failure, Gandhi largely withdrew from the public spotlight until 1930.

between the two groups grew. Muslims were concerned that, as a minority, their voices would not be heard in a Hindu-dominated India. They wanted guaranteed political representation and requested that three Muslim states be established in the Sind, Baluchistan, and the North-West Frontier Territory. These requests were denied, frustrating Muslims and doing little to assuage their fears.

In December of 1928, Congress passed a resolution asking that India be granted Dominion status and that Britain withdraw within a year. The new Labour government in England agreed to grant Dominion status. It further invited the Congress to participate in Round Table discussions on India's future. The meetings, to be held in London, would include British authorities as well as India's princes. Congress, believing that attendance would mean acceding to British terms, boycotted the conference. In the absence of Congress, the Round Table worked out the Dominion status for India. The state would be a democratic federation made up of the British territories and the princely states. The British also agreed to speed up the process of integrating Indians into the government.

In early 1930, Gandhi reentered the political sphere. This time he targeted the so-called Salt Laws, which imposed a tax on salt and prohibited Indians from making their own. In March Gandhi walked 250 miles (402 km) from his home to the town of Dandi on the coast, where he picked up a piece of salt from the beach. His meaning was clear: The English tax what can be obtained for free. Thousands of followers—including, to the chagrin of high-caste Hindus, many untouchables—accompanied Gandhi on the highly publicized march. Ultimately the Raj arrested at least 60,000 people, including Gandhi, for civil disobedience in connection with the Salt Laws. These protesters clogged India's prisons and court system.

For the most part, Muslims stayed out of Gandhi's demonstrations. For many of them, a Hindu state would only mean less representation than they got under the British.

Participants in the Salt March gather sea salt from the beach at Dandi, 1930. Mahatma Gandhi can be seen at left in this photo, with open shirt.

In the fall of 1930, the viceroy, Lord Irwin, asked Gandhi for a meeting. After long and difficult negotiations, the two worked out an agreement. Gandhi agreed to stop the protests and attend a second Round Table discussion in London. In return, 19,000 of Gandhi's followers were released from prison and the manufacture of salt was allowed.

The Second Round Table Conference foundered on the issue of minority participation in government, a subject on which Hindus and Muslims could not agree. The conference broke up in December 1931, and more civil disobedience soon followed in India.

The Third Round Table Conference, which convened in November of the following year, also failed to achieve consensus on a constitution for

India, so the British Parliament took action on that matter. The resulting Government of India Act of 1935 provided for a federal state whose central government would have a two-chamber legislature (with guaranteed Muslim representation). But the provisions establishing the central government would go into effect only after half the states (including the princely states) agreed to join the new country, which did not happen. In addition, the British retained control of foreign policy, defense, and finances, and under certain circumstances the viceroy could act unilaterally regardless of the wishes of the legislature.

With regard to the provinces, the Government of India Act in theory made British-appointed governors answerable to their provincial legislatures. But significant loopholes left open the possibility of unilateral action by governors.

The Indian National Congress and the Muslim League both opposed the Government of India Act, but they had to decide whether to participate in elections for the provincial legislatures or be shut out of provincial governments. They chose to participate. Congress, which was better organized than the Muslim League, turned out more voters and dominated the 1937 polling.

In many areas Congress-controlled provincal governments began handing out political appointments to members and replacing Muslim workers with Hindus. In one state, Bihar, the Hindu majority passed a law banning the killing of cows, an issue the groups had fought over for many years.

Not surprisingly, this turn of events spurred greater membership in the Muslim League, which since 1935 had been led by Mohammed Ali Jinnah. A prominent lawyer, Jinnah had been a member of the Indian National Congress for 30 years and a longtime proponent of Muslim-Hindu cooperation, which he regarded as essential for any viable independent Indian state. Increasingly, however, he viewed cooperation with skepticism.

While Congress continued to demand a fully independent India, the Muslims, led by Jinnah, demanded guaranteed representation to safeguard their interests. All the while, the viceroy was trying without success to bring the princes into a new federal state. No one, it seemed, could fully achieve their goals.

World War II and the "Quit India" Movement

On September 1, 1939, Nazi Germany invaded Poland. Two days later England, joined by its ally France, declared war on Germany. World War II had begun.

Without consulting Indian leaders, the viceroy declared India to be at war with Germany. This rankled leaders of the Indian National Congress, including Mohandas Gandhi and Jawaharlal Nehru, who decided to maintain an official stance of neutrality with regard to the Anglo-German hostilities. The Muslim League, meanwhile, declared its support of the British cause.

The position taken by Congress contributed greatly to the indifference of most Indians toward Britain's plight. But while the Indian public didn't mobilize in support of England, previously constituted Indian units did fight on the British side, especially in North Africa.

Mohammed Ali Jinnah addresses delegates to a Muslim League convention in New Delhi. Formerly a member of the Indian National Congress and an influential voice for Hindu-Muslim cooperation, Jinnah became the leading advocate for an independent Muslim state.

The stakes—for England as well as India—grew immeasurably in 1941, when Germany's ally Japan attacked and overwhelmed British colonies in the Far East such as Malay and Burma. In mid-1942, with the outcome of the war still in the balance and Japanese forces near the Burma-India border, Gandhi and the Indian National Congress spear-headed what came to be called the "Quit India" movement. Unless the British agreed to grant India complete and immediate independence, Congress would organize a massive civil disobedience campaign. On

Jawaharlal Nehru (left) and Mahatma Gandhi share views at the August 1942 conference during which the Indian National Congress adopted the "Quit India" resolution. The British responded to the resolution by arresting the entire Congress leadership, touching off large-scale rioting.

August 9, a day after the "Quit India" resolution was passed, the British authorities moved to arrest Gandhi and the entire Congress leadership. Uncontrolled rioting, acts of sabotage, and arson attacks ensued.

The British response was swift and harsh. Mobs were dispersed with rifle volleys and occasionally even aerial bombing. Protesters were beaten, flogged, and jailed by the tens of thousands. By early 1944 relative calm had been restored, but the strife had claimed the lives of as many as 4,000 people, with up to 10,000 others wounded; more than 1,500 government buildings had been destroyed; and some 330 railroad stations, critical for the movement of troops and wartime supplies, had been damaged or ruined.

It is difficult to gauge the impact of Quit India. Some say that the sheer size of the movement broke the Raj's will to continue ruling India. Others believe that the movement's primary effect was to strengthen the position of those who did not participate, particularly the Muslim League and its leader, Mohammed Ali Jinnah. By this time Jinnah was firmly set on obtaining Pakistan (which he hoped would comprise the Sind, the North-West Frontier Province, Kashmir, Punjab, and Bengal) as an independent state for India's Muslims when the war came to an end.

Endgame

In 1945 Germany and Japan surrendered, bringing World War II to a victorious conclusion for Britain and the Allies. But the conflict had exhausted the British Empire, which could ill afford to plunge resources into a futile effort to hang on to India. By war's end England owed India £1.3 billion for the cost of mobilized troops and equipment, yet the empire's former "crown jewel" no longer held the same economic significance for Britain: India was importing fewer goods from England and selling more to other markets.

In order to gauge public sentiment regarding the future of self-rule, an election was held in 1945. As before, Congress won in largely Hindu areas, and the Muslim League won in the Sind and Bengal. In Punjab, Sikhs, Hindus, and a rival Muslim group known as the Muslim Unionist Alliance kept the Muslim League from gaining a majority. The mood throughout India was anxious, even fearful, as independence approached with the volatile issue of Pakistan unresolved.

In February 1946, a mutiny erupted among Indian sailors aboard the HMIS *Talwar,* and the uprising soon spread to other ships in the Royal Indian Navy. The army was called in to quell the insurrection. As violence raged on the ships and docks, local Communists in Bombay quickly organized a protest of cotton mill workers, and rioting spread throughout the city. British soldiers were deployed along with fighter-bombers to put down the uprising. Congress, deeply disturbed that Communists had managed to direct the revolt, supported the Raj in its counterinsurgency. Within days the situation was under control, but military commanders had reason to worry about the loyalty of their units. More important, the government had to wonder how the military would respond in the event of a large-scale insurrection.

In March a delegation arrived from Britain to again attempt to work out the problem of self-rule and representation. The British still desired a unified India, as did Congress. But Jinnah insisted on the creation of Pakistan, arguing that the Hindu Congress would never build a secular state in which Muslim interests were protected. On May 16 a plan emerged. A centralized government administration would continue to be responsible for foreign policy, defense, and internal communication. Internally, India would be divided into three regions. Group A, containing Madras, Bombay, Orissa, and the United and Central Provinces, would encompass the Congress areas. Group B would contain the Muslim areas of Baluchistan, the North-West Frontier Province, the Sind, and the Punjab. Group C would consist of Bengal and Assam, which were closer to religious parity than any other provinces. Each group was to create its own constitution and then elect representatives to a national forum for a national constitution. Eventually, all the parties agreed to the plan, and the British were hopeful that a workable solution had been found.

But as the delegation returned home, the agreement quickly fell apart. Jawaharlal Nehru, elected president of the Congress, announced that his provinces would do as they pleased. Further, he said, the North-West Frontier Province would never join a region dominated by the Muslim League, and he predicted that Assam would not ally with Bengal. The Muslim League responded to Nehru's declarations by withdrawing from the agreement.

Jinnah had concluded that negotiations with Congress were never going to bear fruit. Whenever he proposed the creation of Pakistan, Congress vehemently opposed the plan. His only option, he believed, was to create his country by force. Jinnah declared August 16 Direct Action Day.

As that date approached, Indians prepared for war, stockpiling weapons and training in private armies. Incidents of intercommunal violence broke out regularly. Uncertain of the loyalty of their men, British commanders did little to intervene.

On August 16 a crowd of Muslims estimated at up to half a million gathered at Calcutta's Ochterlony Monument. Orators whipped the crowd into a frenzy with angry speeches, and at the conclusion of the rally gangs of Muslims went on a killing spree, murdering any Hindus they could find. The police did nothing to stop them.

By the following morning, the northwest section of Calcutta was on fire, and Hindus had begun taking revenge. The military was deployed, but it took six days to restore order. By the end, some 4,000 people were dead.

As refugees fled Calcutta, the killing spread. The horror stories enraged those in outlying areas who then struck against local villages. In Bengal,

(Above) On August 16, 1946, as many as half a million Muslims gathered in Calcutta, answering Jinnah's call "for the Muslim nation to resort to Direct Action to achieve Pakistan, to assert their just rights, to vindicate their honour and to get rid of the present British slavery and the contemplated future Caste-Hindu domination." (Opposite page) Two weeks later, this Calcutta street scene only hinted at the violence that Direct Action Day had unleashed.

Muslims burned Hindu villages and embarked on a terror campaign to convince Hindus to leave. Countless atrocities were committed by both sides.

Nevertheless, on September 2, the interim government was established with Nehru as its prime minister. At first, the Muslim League refused to participate, but on October 26, Jinnah relented. He calculated that representation in the new government would be a step toward the creation of Pakistan.

The situation remained volatile as a new viceroy, Sir Louis Mountbatten, arrived in March 1947 with the mandate of extricating

Britain from India by the deadline of June 30, 1948. Though he was generally more sympathetic toward the perspectives of Gandhi and Nehru, Mountbatten agreed with Jinnah that partition was the only workable solution to India's religiously based strife. Mountbatten and his staff worked feverishly to produce an acceptable partition arrangement. Among the many thorny issues that needed to be worked out was how to divide India's army. Hindus and Muslims had long fought side by side, and the state of their origin had not determined their place in the regiments. A disproportionate number of the men in the army were from the Punjab, an area that was itself in dispute. Dividing the military based on the soldier's place of origin, as simple as it might sound, was not an option. In addition, more than 10,000 British officers would need to be replaced.

Partisans didn't wait to hear the details of Mountbatten's plan. In areas likely to be partitioned, such as Bengal and the Punjab, they initiated violent campaigns of a kind that today might be termed "ethnic cleansing." Recognizing that control of as much of the Punjab as possible would be critical to the economic prospects of Pakistan, members of the Muslim League organized terror attacks on the region's Hindu and Sikh communities, using rape, murder, and arson to drive out as many as possible. Hindus and Sikhs responded in kind.

The situation became so intolerable that both Nehru and Jinnah, who were unable to convince their respective constituencies to stop the slaughter, pleaded with the British to establish martial law and flood the area with troops. In the end, however, restoring order took a backseat to producing a partition plan quickly, as Mountbatten believed that delays in the transfer of power would merely prolong the violence. The deadline for the handover was moved up from June 30, 1948, to August 15, 1947.

By late April 1947, Mountbatten and his staff had crafted a partition plan, dubbed "Plan Balkan," that seemed acceptable to Jinnah as well as the Indian National Congress. But when Mountbatten shared final details of the plan with Nehru, the Congress leader balked at a provision that would grant full independence to all of India's 562 princely states and allow them to decide where their political futures lay. This, Nehru protested, might cause India to regress politically to the pre–British Raj era times when small lords vied for each other's lands. In the end, Plan Balkan had to be rewritten.

Partition and Independence

The rewritten Plan Balkan passed quickly through Parliament and the interim government. In Mountbatten's final plan, Bengal, the Punjab, and the North-West Frontier Province would be allowed to decide their own fate. Bengal voted to split; the western half would join India, and the eastern half would join Pakistan. The Punjab also voted to split, with the western section joining Pakistan and the eastern section becoming part of India. The North-West Frontier Province voted to join Pakistan.

With the future of those areas determined, Mountbatten had only to resolve the question of what to do with the princely states. The princes had long-standing agreements with the British that allowed them to rule their small monarchies without the interference of the Raj. The princes supported the British financially during World War II in the hopes that their autonomy would be respected, but a self-ruled India had no place for small kingdoms.

Jawaharlal Nehru (left) and Mohammed Ali Jinnah (right) are presented details of the British plan for partitioning India. Seated between the Hindu and Muslim leaders at this June 1947 conference is Lord Louis Mountbatten, the British viceroy. Mountbatten's adviser, Lord Ismay, sits in the back.

The princes were essentially told that they had to merge their states into India or Pakistan. Most princes chose India, a few chose Pakistan, but three—the rulers of Jammu and Kashmir, Hyderabad, and Junagadh—declined to join either.

In order to complete partition, borders had to be drawn. A committee of two Muslims, two Hindus, and one English jurist was given five weeks to complete the job. The deliberations were supposed to be secret, in order to minimize conflict before the handover, but information was regularly leaked to party leaders. In particular dispute was an area of irrigation systems in the Punjab around the towns of Firozpur and Gurdaspur. Whoever controlled this area would have control over the water necessary for farming and the only bridge over the river Sutlej. Originally, this area was given to Pakistan, but subsequent pleas to Mountbatten behind closed doors resulted in its reallocation to India.

The transfer of power occurred as planned on August 15, 1947. Mountbatten, who would serve as India's governor-general until 1948, presided over elaborate ceremonies. Jinnah toasted King George VI, the enlightened monarch who had handed over power willingly; George would remain India's official head of state until 1950. All over India, the day was marked with colorful celebrations.

But while direct British rule in India had officially ceased and two independent countries—India and Pakistan—had been born, the decisions of the Boundary Committee establishing the borders of those two countries had not yet been announced. Mountbatten was sure that violence would erupt when the boundaries were made public, so he chose to wait until after the power transfer. In the absence of authoritative information, rumors abounded, and violence again hit the Punjab. British investigations into terrorist activity in the region revealed a sophisticated network of bomb-makers, arsonists, and saboteurs. A Sikh nationalist movement had developed, and it had plans to assassinate Jinnah. The situation had

End of an era: Lord Mountbatten formally announces the transfer of power from Great Britain to independent India and Pakistan, August 15, 1947.

gotten wildly out of hand. Sikh nationalists, Hindus, and Muslims were all bent on war, and there was no longer any force capable of mustering the military strength to contain them.

Violence and the threat of violence spurred mass migrations. After partition, approximately 7 million Muslims crossed from India into Pakistan, with 6 million of them going to West Pakistan. Meanwhile, some 3.5 million Hindus migrated into India from East Pakistan, and 6.5 million Hindus and Sikhs left West Pakistan for Indian territory. Marauding gangs of criminals robbed and killed many migrants; many lives were lost to religiously based violence as well. All told, an estimated 1 million people died trying to cross the borders between India and Pakistan.

Unresolved Issues

In the aftermath of the British withdrawal, partition, and mass migrations between India and Pakistan, the basic outlines of the Subcontinent's political future had been resolved—albeit at a tragic cost in human suffering and with considerable chaos. However, the failure of two large princely states (Kashmir and Hyderabad) to join either India or Pakistan left some questions unanswered. (The relatively small Junagadh had announced its accession to Pakistan on August 15, but Indian pressure soon reversed that decision.)

Pakistan decided not to wait and see what the Hindu **maharaja** of predominantly Muslim Jammu and Kashmir ultimately decided. On October 22, 1947, tribal Pashtun fighters from Pakistan's North-West Frontier Province, probably with the encouragement of the Pakistani government, invaded Kashmir. In the wake of this incursion, under circumstances that are still disputed, the maharaja signed an agreement to join India;

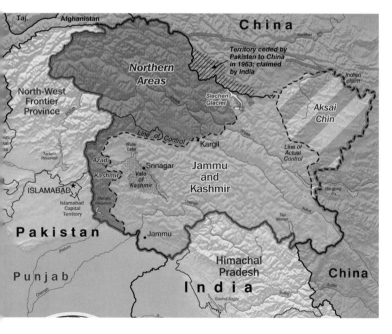

India and Pakistan first clashed over Kashmir in October 1947, just two months after partition. Sixty years later, the status of the predominantly Muslim region remains uncertain.

Pakistan insisted that the Instrument of Accession was not legal, however. Indian army units were deployed, and soon they were battling Pakistani troops who had moved into Kashmir. Fighting in the extremely rugged and remote land continued until a United Nations–brokered cease-fire took effect on January 1, 1949. The jagged cease-fire line, running some 500 miles (805 km) and referred to as the Line of Control, left India in possession of about two-thirds of Kashmir and Pakistan occupying the rest. The UN declared that a plebiscite should be held to determine the wishes of the people of Kashmir, but as of 2006 no such poll had taken place.

Hyderabad, a large state in south-central India, was ruled by Nizam Osman Ali Khan, a Muslim. But about 85 percent of his 16 million subjects were Hindus. Indian leaders considered it essential that Hyderabad be integrated into their country, but for a time they were willing to countenance independence for the princely state as long as its leader promised not to join Pakistan. Various plans for incorporating Hyderabad into India were proposed and rejected. Finally, in September 1948, India decided to settle the issue by force. Its army invaded Hyderabad and quickly defeated the kingdom's armed forces. Hyderabad's territory was later divided among three Indian states.

India's high commissioner in Great Britain, Krishna Menon, signs an oath of allegiance to India's newly effective constitution, January 26, 1950. On that date India officially became a republic.

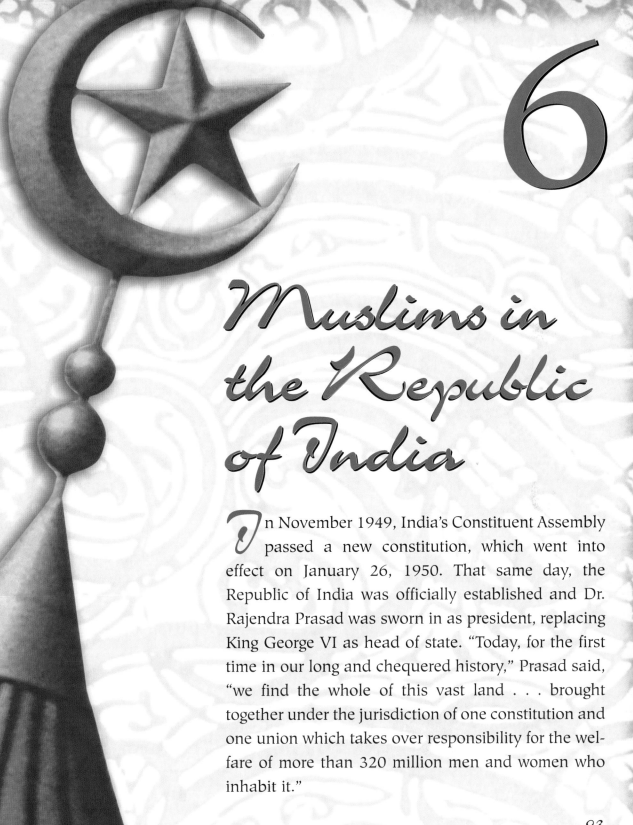

Muslims in the Republic of India

$\mathcal{I}$n November 1949, India's Constituent Assembly passed a new constitution, which went into effect on January 26, 1950. That same day, the Republic of India was officially established and Dr. Rajendra Prasad was sworn in as president, replacing King George VI as head of state. "Today, for the first time in our long and chequered history," Prasad said, "we find the whole of this vast land . . . brought together under the jurisdiction of one constitution and one union which takes over responsibility for the welfare of more than 320 million men and women who inhabit it."

The Indian Constitution, which drew on Western models but also reflected the vision and concerns of Indians, guaranteed all citizens fundamental rights, including freedom of association, freedom of expression, and freedom of religion. The document also guaranteed equal status under the law, even officially abolishing the entrenched custom of "untouchability." Further, it required "adequate safeguards" for India's "minorities, backward and tribal areas, depressed and other backward classes."

Many of the Constitution's more forward-looking provisions bore the imprint of Jawaharlal Nehru. The longtime Congress leader became India's first elected prime minister in 1952 and held the office until his death in 1964. Nehru, arguably the Republic of India's most influential figure— Mahatma Gandhi had been assassinated by a fanatic Hindu nationalist in January 1948—skillfully nurtured the political ideal of a united India with a democratic, secular government.

Today the efforts of Nehru, and of like-minded Indian leaders who came after, must be judged largely successful. Despite a constitutional crisis and suspension of civil rights in 1975–1977 under Nehru's daughter, Prime Minister Indira Gandhi, India's democracy has been stable and enduring. India, unlike many former colonies that gained independence after World War II—and unlike many ethnically and religiously diverse developing states during the late 20th century—has not been ripped apart by civil war.

That said, **sectarian** violence has taken a terrible toll in the Republic of India. Much of the strife pits Hindus against Muslims.

Kashmir

Jammu and Kashmir, India's only Muslim-majority state, has been a tinderbox. In the years following the 1949 cease-fire, Pakistani and Indian troops regularly exchanged artillery and small-arms fire across the Line of Control. In August and September 1965, India and Pakistan fought another full-fledged war in Kashmir, with significant casualties on both sides. Indian and Pakistani units in Kashmir engaged in more limited fighting in 1971, after India intervened in Bangladesh's war of independence from Pakistan.

Even though the Line of Control has functioned as a de facto border for more than five decades, India and Pakistan both lay claim to all 86,000 square miles (223,000 sq km) of "Greater Kashmir," which comprises the Indian state of Jammu and Kashmir and the Pakistani-controlled Azad Kashmir ("Free Kashmir"). The wishes of residents vary. Within Indian-controlled Jammu and Kashmir, many Hindus and Buddhists favor the status quo, although the organization Panun Kashmir demands the creation of a separate state within India for Kashmiri Pandits (Hindus of a higher caste, who have been displaced by violence in Kashmir). Muslims in Indian-controlled Kashmir are more likely to advocate union with Pakistan or complete independence.

Indian Kashmiri residents are escorted across the Line of Control, November 17, 2005; they had been trapped in Pakistan-controlled Kashmir by a devastating earthquake that struck on October 8, 2005. India responded to the earthquake by offering Pakistan humanitarian aid—a sign, many observers believed, of improving relations between the two longtime enemies.

In 1989 an armed insurgency against Indian rule erupted in the densely populated and predominantly Muslim Vale of Kashmir, or Kashmir valley. Resentment had been building in the valley since 1987, when Muslim political parties charged that state legislative elections had been fraudulent, and the pro-India authorities responded to the criticism by arresting Muslim leaders. At the very least, Pakistan lent moral support to the insurgents; many analysts found credible India's repeated charges that Pakistan was arming and training the rebels as well.

International observers suggest that initially the Kashmir insurgency was mainly a secular nationalist movement, but during the 1990s it came to be dominated by radical Islamists. Many were mujahideen, or Islamic holy warriors, who had fought against the Soviet occupation of Afghanistan during the 1980s.

According to the Associated Press, the violence in Kashmir claimed an estimated 66,000 lives between 1989 and September 2005. While some of these casualties came in clashes between rebels and Indian army troops, most of the dead were civilians. Islamic militant groups carried out a series of bombings, assassinations, and arson attacks directed at Hindus and moderate Muslims. The Indian security forces responded harshly, according to international human rights organizations. Human Rights Watch accused the security forces, along with paramilitary groups under their direction, of tactics such as the arbitrary detention of large numbers of Muslims, torture, and murder. The ongoing violence displaced 650,000 Kashmiri residents.

Events in late 2001 and 2002 pushed India and Pakistan—both of which now possessed nuclear weapons—to the brink of another war. On October 1, 2001, a suicide bombing and assault on Jammu and Kashmir's parliament building in the summer capital, Srinagar, killed 40 people and wounded 75; India blamed Pakistan for the attack. Then, on December 13, five young men later identified as members of the Kashmiri Muslim terrorist organization Lashkar-e-Taiba attacked India's Parliament in New Delhi, which had adjourned for the day only minutes earlier. In a 45-minute gun battle with police, the terrorists killed 10 before themselves being killed. An Islamic group claimed responsibility for the attack, and India again charged that Pakistan had sponsored the terrorists, but Pakistan's president, Pervez Musharraf, denied any involvement by his country.

Guerrilla attacks in Kashmir escalated in May 2002, and nearly a million Indian and Pakistani troops faced each other across the border. War was averted, however, and despite continuing attacks in Kashmir (including the

Hindu youths carry a friend wounded during sectarian rioting in the Mau district of Uttar Pradesh, October 2005. The violence erupted after Hindus conducted a religious ceremony in a predominantly Muslim area.

March 2003 massacre of 24 Hindus in the village of Nadimarg and a grenade attack on a crowded market in Shopian in July 2003), tensions between India and Pakistan were gradually reduced. A cease-fire across the Line of Control took effect later in the year, and India announced plans to normalize relations with Pakistan. Road and rail links were also opened between the Indian and Pakistani areas of Kashmir.

Peace talks began in early 2004. While the status of Kashmir remained unresolved on the eve of high-level talks in January 2006, observers hoped for a breakthrough that might end the violence once and for all.

Causes of Communal Violence in India

It might be argued that, because of its Muslim-majority population, the competing territorial claims of Pakistan and India, and its still-unresolved political future, Kashmir represents a uniquely intractable situation for Hindu-Muslim relations. However, deadly violence between India's Hindu and Muslim communities has by no means been confined to Kashmir. Founded a half-century ago amid sectarian strife, the Republic of India has suffered periodic spasms of communal bloodletting ever since.

Several factors help explain the persistence of religiously based violence in officially secular India. Among some Hindus, resentment lingers over the perceived destruction of Hindu culture during the centuries of Muslim rule. In certain quarters Muslims are also blamed for the partition of the Subcontinent and are suspected of harboring sympathies for India's enemy Pakistan. Some Hindus resent what they regard as the government's preferential treatment of Muslims (and other minority groups), including separate electorates to guarantee minority representation and government funding of Muslim religious schools. For their part, many Muslims claim that they suffer discrimination in the educational system, in the workplace, and in the justice system. Both Hindus and Muslims chafe at the treatment of their co-religionists in Kashmir.

The rise of two movements—Islamic fundamentalism and Hindu nationalism—has coincided with, and probably fanned, increased communal distrust and resentment in India. Although India today is not known as a breeding ground for Islamic fundamentalism, the Darul Uloom madrassa (Islamic religious school) in the town of Deoband, established in 1867, served as an important center for conservative Muslim thought. The resulting Deobandi philosophy strongly opposed Western influences, defined the primary duty of Muslims as allegiance to Islam rather than allegiance to a nation-state, and espoused a highly restrictive role for women. The Deobandi perspective, influential in Pakistan as well

The Darul Uloom madrassa, founded in the northern Indian town of Deoband in 1867, became an important center of Islamic fundamentalism. The conservative Deobandi philosophy has been particularly influential in Pakistan and Afghanistan. This photo of Darul Uloom students was taken in 2004.

as in Afghanistan during the Taliban regime, is believed to have provided inspiration for some Islamic terrorists in India.

Seeds of a resurgent Hindu nationalism were planted as early as the mid-1960s, when Shiv Sena—a Hindu political party with an anti-immigrant (and ultimately anti-Muslim) message—formed in Bombay, capital of the state of Maharashtra. But for some time that message did not play particularly well on the national political stage, which was dominated by the mainstream Congress Party until 1989. Following the 1989 elections, however, a coalition of opposition parties, including the Hindu-nationalist Bharatiya Janata Party (BJP), ruled briefly. Thereafter the fortunes of the BJP rose steadily. The 1991 elections brought BJP governments to four states, including India's largest, Uttar Pradesh. In 1998 the BJP came to power in the central government.

The BJP's platform, which appealed to Hindu villagers and middle-class citizens resentful of Muslim "special rights," centered on restoring Hinduism to its "proper" place in Indian society and was largely anti-minority, and especially anti-Muslim. The BJP national government even began rewriting school textbooks to give history a more Hindu slant—omitting, for example, the fact that Mahatma Gandhi was assassinated by a Hindu fanatic.

India's Hindu-Muslim animosity has deep roots, and obviously it would be a mistake to place too much blame on the BJP and its Hindu nationalist allies for flare-ups of religious violence beginning in the 1990s. But, critics charge, BJP rhetoric exacerbated old hatreds, and when some of the worst rioting and killing since the partition era exploded in Gujarat in 2002, the BJP was slow to restore order.

Flashpoint

The 2002 rioting in Gujarat was fueled by a long-running conflict in Ayodhya, Uttar Pradesh. That conflict, involving a contested religious site, is in many respects emblematic of the troubled and tangled history of Muslim-Hindu relations in India.

Hindus consider Ayodhya the birthplace of the important god Rama, so for them it is revered ground. During the Mughal era, however, Mir Baqi, a nobleman from Babur's court, constructed a mosque, the Babri Masjid, in Ayodhya. The mosque may have been constructed on the site of an 11th-century Hindu temple to Rama, or the temple may have simply been topped with a dome to transform it into a Muslim place of worship. In 1857 a Hindu priest built an altar in the compound. Hindus and Muslims both worshiped there until the British separated them with a wall in 1859. During countrywide Hindu-Muslim riots in 1934, Hindus damaged the mosque. In 1949, after a Rama idol was placed inside and Hindus seized the building, the government closed it.

In 1983 the BJP and the militant group Vishwa Hindu Parishad (VHP) campaigned to raze the Babri Masjid and build a Hindu temple at the site. The Sangh Parivar—a Hindu political movement that brought together the BJP, VHP, and affiliated social and cultural organizations—collected 167,000 bricks from around the world for the Rama temple, and in 1989 Hindus held a ceremony and dug a pit to lay the foundation stone. This triggered Muslim-Hindu riots that killed about 600. The Muslim Babri Masjid Action Committee formed to oppose Sangh Parivar's plans, and the Congress government decided to send the case to India's Supreme Court for adjudication.

In 1990 BJP leader Lal Krishna Advani led a five-week procession to Ayodhya in support of the Rama temple construction. More than 100,000 Hindu pilgrims assembled at Ayodhya, and on October 30 at least 20,000 of them stormed the mosque. Police efforts to contain the crowd, along with ensuing Hindu-Muslim riots, claimed the lives of nearly 250 people.

In July 1992, construction ceremonies began on the Rama temple, though the Babri Masjid itself was not disturbed at that time. In

Militant Hindus storm the Babri Masjid, October 1990. The 16th-century mosque is located in Ayodhya, Uttar Pradesh, which Hindus consider the birthplace of the god Rama.

December, however, an estimated 300,000 Hindus wielding spades, crowbars, axes, and shovels demolished the mosque.

The incident triggered nationwide rioting, during which more than 2,000 people, mostly Muslims, were killed. Amid the unrest, Prime Minister V. P. Singh resigned, pleading with all Indians to show tolerance toward those of a different faith. "Religion is the lamp of the soul," Singh said. "Let it light your way. Do not use it to ignite the flames of hatred. If you do so, the Temple of Mother India will be reduced to ashes."

But Singh's words were not heeded. Between 1992 and 2002, some 4,000 people were killed in violence over the Babri Masjid.

The final status of the Babri Masjid complex remained legally unresolved, though the Supreme Court issued an order prohibiting construction on the site pending a definitive decision. In January 2002, despite that order, the VHP informed Prime Minister Atal Behari Vajpayee—leader of the Hindu nationalist BJP—that it would start construction on the Rama temple on March 15 if the matter was not resolved by then. In February some 15,000 Hindu nationalists traveled to Ayodhya for a rally there.

During the early-morning hours of February 27, several hundred of these demonstrators were returning home to Ahmadabad, Gujarat's largest city and financial hub, aboard an express train. Shortly after dawn, the train arrived at the Godhra railway station on the Gujarat–Madhya Pradesh border. A group of armed Muslims waiting on the platform boarded the train, which they later forced to stop near a largely Muslim village.

By nightfall on February 27, 2002, when this photo was taken, the flames that burned to death 59 Hindus in a train car near Godhra had been extinguished. But the deadly rioting in Gujarat was only beginning. Over the following six weeks, more than 2,000 people—mostly Muslims—would be killed, and 100,000 would be left homeless by the violence.

Local residents, many wielding swords and crowbars, had assembled there. Precisely what happened next is disputed, but Hindu witnesses reported that the mob doused with gasoline a carriage packed with Hindu women and children, then set it ablaze. Fifty-nine people were burned alive.

Only hours after the train massacre, Hindus in Ahmadabad began retaliating. Hindu mobs rampaged through the city's Muslim Old Quarter, burning homes and businesses and mercilessly slaughtering Muslims. Outlying areas of Ahmadabad were quickly engulfed by the rioting, which the local police force seemed unable or unwilling to quell.

The mayhem spread throughout the prosperous state of Gujarat. More than two dozen major cities and towns were torn by an orgy of murder, rape, looting, and arson as the Hindu and Muslim communities lashed out at each other with unrestrained fury. Unlike previous sectarian riots in India—which generally did not last for more than a few days—the rioting in Gujarat continued at a fever pitch for six weeks, then sputtered on in isolated areas. Over 2,000 people were killed, and an additional 100,000 left homeless, by the violence. The overwhelming majority of the victims were Muslims.

Another Vision

For outsiders, it was perhaps easy to view the horrifying carnage in Gujarat as merely the latest flare-up in a never-ending cycle of violence within a country whose major religious groups could not live together peacefully—and would never be able to live together peacefully. Such a view is inaccurate, however. The reality is that, in much of India most of the time, Indians and Muslims do coexist in a relatively harmonious fashion. In his 2002 book *Ethnic Conflict and Civic Life: Hindus and Muslims in India*, author Ashutosh Varshney examined sectarian rioting in India for the period 1950–1995. Varshney concluded that the violence was largely

Thirsting for revenge for the Godhra train massacre, a Hindu mob marches toward a Muslim section of Ahmadabad, March 1, 2002.

confined to 4 of India's 28 states. Beyond that, he found that the violence was concentrated in urban areas. Specifically, 30 cities produced 70 percent of the Hindu-Muslim violence, and just 8 of these cities—including New Delhi, Mumbai, and Kolkata (formerly Calcutta)—accounted for nearly half of all deaths. Although a significant proportion of India's population continues to live in rural villages, sectarian killings in rural areas constituted only about 3 percent of the national total, according to Varshney's study.

The more optimistic view of India as a broadly tolerant society seemed to gain confirmation in the months after the Gujarat bloodletting. Prime Minister Vajpayee's nomination of a Muslim, A. P. J. Abdul Kalam, as the

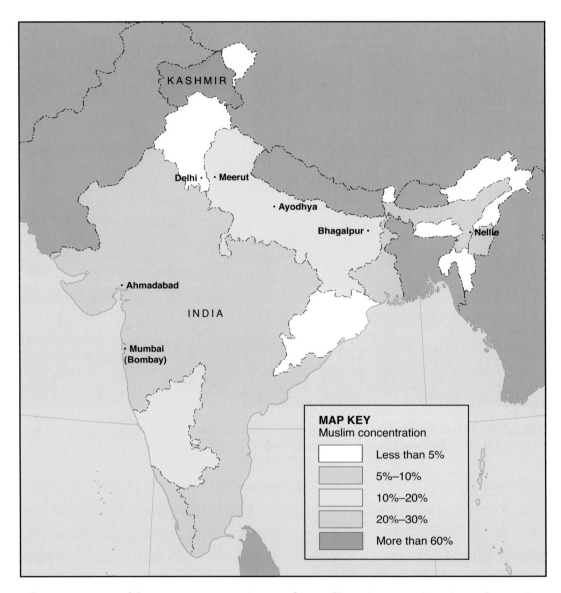

MAP KEY
Muslim concentration

- Less than 5%
- 5%–10%
- 10%–20%
- 20%–30%
- More than 60%

The presence of large concentrations of Muslims in a region is at best size an imperfect predictor of Hindu-Muslim violence. Kashmir, Uttar Pradesh, and Assam, states in northern or northeastern India, all have Muslim populations well above the national average of 13.4 percent, and all have suffered recurring sectarian bloodletting. Yet in the western state of Gujarat, where some of the deadliest rioting since partition has occurred, only about 9 percent of the people follow Islam. And in the southwestern state of Kerala, nearly one in four residents is a Muslim, yet there—as in the rest of southern India—religiously based violence is uncommon.

BJP's presidential candidate sparked celebrations throughout India and even prompted an endorsement from the opposition Congress Party. On July 25, 2002, Kalam won a landslide victory, garnering 89 percent of the popular vote. His popularity among Hindus as well as Muslims was seen as an opportunity for unity. Of the man who would occupy India's highest office, *Newsweek* wrote, "His dream now is to make India a 'secure and developed' nation, with tolerance as the bedrock of public discourse."

Dissatisfaction with the BJP's failure to stop the bloody rioting in Gujarat helped lead, two years later, to the Hindu nationalist party's defeat in national elections, despite last-minute attempts to soften its radical stance and woo Muslim voters. "I think what happened in Gujarat," Prime Minister Manmohan Singh, a Sikh, told an interviewer in January 2005, "was a big shock to our people. I think it's not wrong to say that the May 2004 elections were a reaffirmation of the hearts and minds of the people of India."

Most observers agree that sectarian tensions in India have declined in the years after the 2002 rioting (despite incidents such as the August 25, 2003, Islamic terrorist bombings in Mumbai's business district, which claimed 52 lives and injured more than 200). Several factors might explain this lessening of Hindu-Muslim friction: India's robust economy, which has been growing at an annual rate of 6.8 percent since 1994, lifting many citizens out of poverty and expanding the middle class; better relations with Pakistan, and even the prospect of a resolution to the Kashmir situation; and the electoral defeat of the BJP.

Nevertheless, analysts suggest that an undercurrent of disaffection continues to exist among many of India's 138 million Muslims. Various social and economic indicators suggest that Muslims are not sharing equally in India's recent progress: Muslims have a lower average income than Hindus (as well as other minority groups), suffer higher unemployment, and have a higher rate of illiteracy. Muslims hold only 3 percent of

A. P. J. Abdul Kalam, a Muslim, won a landslide victory in July 2002 to become India's president. Some observers viewed the election results, which came on the heels of the Gujarat rioting, as a repudiation of Hindu-nationalist politics—and as cause for optimism about the future of Hindu-Muslim relations in the world's largest democracy.

government jobs, and, Muslims say, Hindus shut them out of many private-sector positions as well. Perhaps more significantly, Muslims in some parts of India have expressed doubts about whether their government can guarantee them a reasonable degree of security in the face of Hindu passions, or whether the Hindu-dominated police and courts are interested in justice when Muslims are victimized by Hindus. Statistics suggest that these doubts are not unwarranted: in the Gujarat rioting of 2002, for example, official records indicate that 85 percent of the victims were Muslims. Yet only a handful of Hindus have yet been prosecuted for the crimes, and convictions have been rarer still.

For their part, some Hindus have expressed fears about India's growing Muslim population. Birthrates among Muslims have been outstripping birthrates among Hindus, and certain Hindu nationalists have suggested that this threatens their culture.

Sixty years after achieving independence, multicultural, multiethnic India remains intact. But it appears to have a long way to go before its major religious groups live together in harmony.

Chronology

ca. 2600 B.C.	Beginning of the Indus Valley civilization (also known as the Harappan culture).
ca. 1500 B.C.	Hinduism develops in India.
6th century B.C.	Jainism and Buddhism develop from Hinduism.
3rd century B.C.	Ashoka, ruler of the Mauryan Empire, conquers much of India and spreads Buddhism.
A.D. 320–550	The Gupta Empire rules northern India in what is considered the golden age of Hindu culture.
711	The Muslim governor of Iraq invades the Sind and sweeps into the Indus Valley.
ca. 1000	Mahmud of Ghazni launches the first in a series of destructive raids into India.
1206	Qutb-ud-din-Aybak proclaims himself the first sultan of Delhi.
1398	The Turkish conqueror Timur Lenk sacks Delhi, reducing the Delhi Sultanate to a local power.
1526	Babur defeats the last Delhi sultan, Ibrahim Lodi, and founds the Mughal dynasty.
1556	Akbar the Great becomes the Mughal ruler; his reign lasts nearly 50 years.
1600	The British East India Company is chartered in London.
1627	Shah Jahan, builder of the Taj Mahal, becomes Mughal emperor.
1658	Aurangzeb, considered the last powerful Mughal emperor, takes the throne.
1757	The East India Company general Robert Clive wins the Battle of Plassey, gaining control in Bengal and marking the beginning of the British Raj.
1857	The Indian Rebellion, also known as the Sepoy Mutiny, breaks out among Indian professional soldiers employed by the British East India Company.

1858	The East India Company is abolished, and the British Crown assumes direct authority over India.
1885	The Indian National Congress forms.
1905	To ease tensions between Muslims and Hindus, the British partition Bengal; Hindu outrage eventually forces the partition to be annulled in 1911.
1906	The All-India Muslim League is formed.
1909	The Government of India Act, also known as the Morley-Minto Reforms, provides for limited elections.
1919	At least 379 Sikh civilians are killed in Amritsar in the Jallianwala Bagh massacre.
1920	Mohandas K. Gandhi launches a campaign of peaceful noncooperation with British rule.
1930	Gandhi and thousands of followers protest the Salt Laws.
1942	In the midst of World War II, the Indian National Congress spearheads the "Quit India" movement.
1947	On August 15 the British hand over control, and independent India and Pakistan are created; mass migrations and much violence accompany partition; India and Pakistan fight over Kashmir.
1950	With the adoption of a new constitution, India becomes a sovereign republic.
1965	India and Pakistan again go to war over Kashmir.
1992	After years of escalating tensions, a Hindu mob demolishes the Babri Masjid in Ayodhya.
2001	Terrorist attacks in Kashmir and on India's Parliament push India and Pakistan to the brink of war.
2002	Six weeks of deadly sectarian rioting wracks Gujarat following the massacre of Hindus returning by train from Ayodhya.
2006	India and Pakistan hold talks in January in an effort to resolve the status of Kashmir.

Glossary

amir—a Muslim ruler, chief, or commander.

caste—a hereditary social class in Hindu India.

dhimmi—a non-Muslim given protected status under Muslim rule.

Indian Subcontinent—a large projecting landmass in South Asia south the Himalaya Mountains; usually said to include the countries of India, Pakistan, and Bangladesh.

jizya—a special tax levied on non-Muslims.

majaraja—an Indian prince ranking above a raja.

nawab—a provincial governor of the Mughal Empire.

princely state—any of the numerous semi-independent monarchies on the Indian Subcontinent that were never formally incorporated into British India but that were subject to British influence.

Raj—the name given to British rule in India.

raja—an Indian prince or ruler.

Rajputs—high-caste Hindu warriors who ruled many small kingdoms in India.

satyagraha—a campaign for social and political justice through the use of nonviolent civil disobedience.

sectarian—relating to religious groups or sects.

sepoys—Indian professional soldiers employed by the British.

zamindars—feudal landlords in British India who paid the government a fixed sum.

David, Saul. *The Indian Mutiny, 1857*. London: Viking, 2003.

Dunn, Ross E. *The Adventures of Ibn Battuta: A Muslim Traveler of the 14th Century*. Berkeley: University of California Press, reprint edition, 1990.

Kalam, A. P. J. Abdul. *Wings of Fire: An Autobiography*. Hyderabad: South Asia Books, 1999.

Keay, John. *India, a History*. Boston: Atlantic Monthly Press, 2000.

Koch, Ebba. *Mughal Architecture: An Outline of Its History and Development (1526–1858)*. New Delhi: Oxford University Press, 2002.

———. *Mughal Art and Imperial Ideology: Collected Essays*. New Delhi: Oxford University Press, 2001.

Lapierre, Dominique, and Larry Collins. *Freedom at Midnight*. New Delhi: Vikas Publishing House, 2001.

Nehru, Jawaharlal. *The Discovery of India*. New York: Oxford University Press, reissue of 1946 edition, 1990.

Rai, Mridu. *Hindu Rulers, Muslim Subjects: Islam, Rights, and the History of Kashmir*. Princeton, N.J.: Princeton University Press, 2004.

Sachau, Dr. Edward C. *Alberuni's India*. New Delhi: Rupa & Co., 2002.

Tharoor, Shashi. *Nehru: A Biography*. New York: Arcade Publishing, 2003.

Varshney, Ashutosh. *Ethnic Conflict and Civic Life: Hindus and Muslims in India*. New Haven, Conn.: Yale University Press, 2002.

Zakaria, Rafiq. *The Man Who Divided India: An Insight into Jinnah's Leadership and Its Aftermath*. Mumbai, India: Popular Prakashan, 2001.

Internet Resources

http://www.cia.gov/cia/publications/factbook/geos/in.html

The CIA World Factbook's India page.

http://www.indiacgny.org

The official website of the Consulate General of India in New York covers India's economy, culture, tourism, news, speeches, and more.

http://timesofindia.indiatimes.com/cms.dll/html/uncomp/ default?

The electronic version of an English-language daily Indian newspaper.

www.jktourism.org

This site focuses on information and photos from the Jammu-Kashmir region.

http://www.flonnet.com

An English-language national Indian magazine with photos and articles.

http://pmindia.nic.in

This official site boasts many photographs, along with press releases and the text of speeches.

http://pib.nic.in

The website of the government of India's Press Information Bureau.

Advani, Lal Krishna, 101
Afghanistan, 33, *34*, 36, *99*, 100
Agra, 45, 48
Ahmadabad, *66*, 103–104, *105*
Akbar (son of Aurangzeb), 51
Akbar the Great, 41, 43–46, *52*
Ala-ud-Din, 37
Alamgir ("World Conqueror"). *See*
   Aurangzeb (son of Shah Jahan)
Ali Vardi Khan (governor of Bengal),
   56
All-India Muslim League. *See* Muslim
   League
Anwar-ud-Din, 54, 55
Ashoka (Mauryan Empire king), 24
Aurangzeb (son of Shah Jahan), 50–51
Ayodhya, 100–103
Azad Kashmir ("Free Kashmir"), 95

Babri Masjid (mosque), 101–103
Babur, 42–43
Bahadur Shah (Mughal emperor), 62,
   64
Baluchistan, 32, 76
Bangladesh, 13, 14, 95
Baqi, Mir, 101
Battle of Badr, 31
Battle of Buxar, 58, *59*
Battle of Khandwa, 43
Battle of Panipat
   First, 43
   Second, 44
Battle of Plassey, 57–58
   See also British East India Company
Bayram Khan, 44
Bengal, 37, 44, 70, 82–84, 86–87
   and the British East India
      Company, 56–58

Bhagwan Das, 44
Bharatiya Janata Party (BJP),
   100–103, 107
Bihar (state), 14, 78
Al-Biruni, Muhammad ibn-Ahmad, 34,
   36
Bombay. *See* Mumbai (Bombay)
British East India Company, *52*
   abolishment of the, 63
   founding of the, 53–54
   revolts against the, 56–58
   rivalry of the, with France, 54–56,
      58
   See also British Raj
British Raj
   after the Indian Rebellion, 64–67
   establishment of the, 58–61
   and Indian movement for self-rule,
      69–86
   and the Indian Rebellion, 61–64
   origins of the, 57–59
   See also British East India Company
Buddhism, 17, 24

Calcutta (Kolkata), 54, 56–57, 63,
   83–84, 105
caste system, *22*, 23
   See also Hinduism
Chandra Singh, 55
Clive, Robert, 55–58
Compagnie des Indes Orientales,
   54–56
   See also British East India
      Company
Constitution (Indian), 93–94
culture and arts, 15, 46, 50
Curzon (Lord), 65

Numbers in **bold italic** refer to captions.

Index

Dandi, 76, **77**
Darul Uloom madrassa, 99–100
Deccan Plateau, 14
Delhi, 62, 63, 64
Delhi Sultanate, 36–39, 42–43
Deoband, 99
Direct Action Day, 83–84
Dravidians (ethnic group), 15, 18
Dyer, Rex, 73–74

East Bengal (state), 70
    See also Bengal
East India Company. See British East
    India Company
England. See British Raj
Ethnic Conflict and Civic Life
    (Varshney), 104–105
ethnic groups, 15, 18

Fatehpur Sikri, 45–46
Firuz Shah (Delhi sultan), 37–38
five pillars (of Islam), 31
France, 54–56, 58

Gandhi, Indira, 94
Gandhi, Mohandas Karamchand,
    72–75, 79, 85
        assassination of, 94, 100
        and the "Quit India" movement,
        80–81
        and the Salt Laws, 76–77
Ganges River, 14, **16**
gardens, 43, 47
Genghis Khan, 39, 42
geographic regions, 14–15
Ghazni, 33, 36
Gobind Singh (Sikh guru), 51
Government of India Act of 1935, 78
Government of India Act of 1919
    (Montagu-Chelmsford Reforms), 71

Government of India Act of 1909
    (Morley-Minto Reforms), 70–71
Gujarat, 44, 72
    rioting in, 100–104, **105**, 107
Gupta Empire, 25

Harappan culture (Indus Valley civi-
    lization), 17–18
Harsha (king), 25, 27
Himalaya Mountains, 14–15
Hindu-Muslim conflicts, 33–34, 37,
    51, 98–100
        and Direct Action Day violence,
        83–84
    future of, 104–108
    and Gujarat rioting, 100–104, **105**,
        107
    in Jammu and Kashmir, 94–98
    and Pakistan, 82–91
    during the reign of Akbar the Great,
        44–45
    during the reign of Aurangzeb, 51
    and self-rule movement, 69–70,
        75–76
Hinduism, **14**, 15, 18–25, 61
    and the caste system, **22**, 23
    See also Hindu-Muslim conflicts
Human Rights Watch, 96
Humayun, 43
Hyderabad (princely state), 37, 88,
    89–91

Ibrahim Lodi (Delhi sultan), 42–43
independence, 86–91, 93–94
    and Indian movement for self-rule,
        69–86
India
    establishment of, as independent
        republic, 86–91, **92**, 93–94
    ethnic groups, 15, 18

geographic regions, 13–15
languages, 15
maps, *35*, *68*, *90*, *106*
population, *12*, 13
See also Pakistan
India Act of 1784, 60
Indian National Congress, 69, 70, 72,
  74, 78–79, 81–83, 86, 100, 107
  and the "Quit India" movement,
    80–81
  See also Muslim League
Indian Rebellion, 61–64
  See also British Raj
Indo-Aryans (ethnic group), 15, 18
Indo-Gangetic Plain, 14
Indus Valley civilization (Harappan
  culture), 17–18
Irwin (Lord), 77
Islam, 15–16, 20
  and the Delhi Sultanate, 36–39,
    42–43
  founding of, 27–32
  and the Mughal Empire, 41–51, 53
  spread of, to the Indian
    Subcontinent, 32–33
  See also Hindu-Muslim conflicts

Jahanara (daughter of Shah Jahan), 47
Jahangir (son of Akbar the Great),
  46–47, *48*
Jainism, 17, 24
Jaipal (king), 33
Jalal-ud-din Muhammad. *See* Akbar
  the Great
Jallianwala Bagh massacre, 73–74
Jama Masjid, 47–48
Jammu and Kashmir, 14, *32*, 88, 89,
  94–98
    See also Hindu-Muslim conflicts
Jinnah, Mohammed Ali, 78–79, 81,

82–86, *87*, 88
Junagadh (princely state), 88, 89

Kaaba, *26*, 28, 29
Kalam, A. P. J. Abdul, 105, 107, *108*
Kannauj, 33
Karnataka, 54, 55
Kashmir, 44
  See also Jammu and Kashmir
Khadija, 28
Khalifat Movement, 71–72
Khan, Nizam Osman Ali, 91
Khurram (son of Jahangir). *See* Shah
  Jahan
Kolkata (Calcutta). *See* Calcutta
  (Kolkata)
Koran. *See* Qur'an (Koran)

languages, 15
Lashkar-e-Taiba (terrorist organiza-
  tion), 96–97
Line of Control, 91, 94–95, 98
  See also Pakistan

Madhya Pradesh (state), 14, 43
Madras, 54
Maha Kumbh Mela (festival), *14*
Mahavira ("the Great Hero"), 24
Mahmud (of Ghazni), 33–36
maps, *35*, *68*, *90*, *106*
Marathas, 50, 51, 60
Mathura, 33
Mauryan Empire, 24
Mecca, *26*, 27–29, 30–31
Medina (Yathrib), 29–30
Menon, Krishna, *92*
Mildenhall, John, *52*
Mir Jafar (nawab of Bengal), 57–58
Mir Kasim (nawab of Bengal), 58
Mohandas Karamchand Gandhi. *See*

Index

Gandhi, Mohandas Karamchand
Morari Rao (Maratha chief), 55
Mountbatten, Louis, 84–88, **89**
Mughal Empire, 41–42, 53
    under Akbar the Great, 43–46, **52**
    under Aurangzeb, 50–51
    founding of the, 42–43
    under Shah Jahan, 47–50
Muhammad, **26**, 28–31
Muhammad (of Ghur), 36
Müller, Max, 18
Mumbai (Bombay), 12, 54, 100, 105
Mumtaz Mahal (wife of Shah Jahan), **40**, 48
Musharraf, Pervez, 97
Muslim League, 70, 78–79, 81–84, 86
    See also Indian National Congress
Muslim Unionist Alliance, 82
Muzafar Jang (Deccan ruler), 55

Nadimarg, 98
Nana Sahib, 63, 64
Nehru, Jawaharlal, 79, **80**, 83, 84–86, **87**, 94
New Delhi, 105
Nizam-ul-Mulk (Deccan ruler), 55
North-West Frontier Province, 76, 83, 86–87, 90–91
Nur Jahan (wife of Jahangir), 46–47

Pakistan, 13, 14, 81, 82–91
    and violence in Jammu and Kashmir, 94–98
    See also India
Pande, Mangal (sepoy), 62
Panun Kashmir (organization), 95
Plan Balkan, 86
population
    India, **12**, 13
    Muslim, in India, 15–16

Prasad, Rajendra, 93
princely states, **68**, 87–91
Punjab, 42, 44, 61, 70, 82, 86–87, 89
    rioting in, 73–74

"Quit India" movement, 80–81
    See also Indian National Congress
Qur'an (Koran), 28, **29**
Qutb-ud-din-Aybak (Delhi sultan), 36–37

Raja Sambhaji (Maratha king), 51
Raja Todar Mal, 44
Rajputs (Hindu warrior caste), 36, 43, 44
Rana Sanga (Rajput ruler), 43
Raziyya (sultan), 37
Regulating Act, 60
reincarnation, 20–21
    See also Hinduism
Republic of India. See India
Rowlatt Acts, 72

Saladat Jang (Deccan ruler), 55
Salt Laws, 76, **77**
Sangh Parivar (political movement), 101
self-rule, Indian, 69–86
    See also independence
Sepoy Mutiny. See Indian Rebellion
Shah Alam II, 58, **59**
Shah Jahan, **40**, 47–50
Shahaji (raja), 55
Shams-ud-din Iltemish (sultan), 37
Sher Khan (king of Bengal), 43
Shiv Sena (political party), 100
Shuja-ud Daula (nawab of Awadh), 58
Sikhism, 17, 51
Sind, 32–33, 44, 61, 76, 82
Singh, Manmohan, 107

Singh, V. P., 102
Siraj-ud Daula (nawab of Bengal),
56–58
Sivaji (Marathas leader), 50
Smyth, Carmichael, 62
Somnath, 33–34
Subuktigin (of Ghazni), 33
Sufism, 45

Taj Mahal, *40*, 41, 47, 48–49
Ta'rikh al-Hind (History of India), 34,
36
Tegh Bahadur (Sikh guru), 51
Timur Lenk (Tamerlane), 39, 42
ibn Tughlaq, Muhammad, 37
Tulsi Das (poet), 46

Utbi, 33–34
Uttar Pradesh (state), 14, *97*, 100

Vajpayee, Atal Behari, 103, 105
Varshney, Ashutosh, 104–105
Vedas, 19, 24
See also Hinduism
Vedic (Hindu) culture, 18–19
Vijayanagar kingdom, 37, *38*
Vishwa Hindu Parishad (VHP), 101,
103

West Bengal (state), 14, 70
See also Bengal
Wolpert, Stanley, 37
World War I, 71
World War II, 79–81

Yathrib (Medina), 29–30

Zahir-ud-din Muhammad. *See* Babur

Picture Credits

The **FOREIGN POLICY RESEARCH INSTITUTE (FPRI)** served as editorial consultants for the GROWTH AND INFLUENCE OF ISLAM IN THE NATIONS OF ASIA AND CENTRAL ASIA series. FPRI is one of the nation's oldest "think tanks." The Institute's Middle East Program focuses on Gulf security, monitors the Arab-Israeli peace process, and sponsors an annual conference for teachers on the Middle East, plus periodic briefings on key developments in the region.

Among the FPRI's trustees is a former Secretary of State and a former Secretary of the Navy (and among the FPRI's former trustees and interns, two current Undersecretaries of Defense), not to mention two university presidents emeritus, a foundation president, and several active or retired corporate CEOs.

The scholars of FPRI include a former aide to three U.S. Secretaries of State, a Pulitzer Prize–winning historian, a former president of Swarthmore College and a Bancroft Prize–winning historian, and two former staff members of the National Security Council. And the FPRI counts among its extended network of scholars— especially its Inter-University Study Groups—representatives of diverse disciplines, including political science, history, economics, law, management, religion, sociology, and psychology.

DR. HARVEY SICHERMAN is president and director of the Foreign Policy Research Institute in Philadelphia, Pennsylvania. He has extensive experience in writing, research, and analysis of U.S. foreign and national security policy, both in government and out. He served as Special Assistant to Secretary of State Alexander M. Haig Jr. and as a member of the Policy Planning Staff of Secretary of State James A. Baker III. Dr. Sicherman was also a consultant to Secretary of the Navy John F. Lehman Jr. (1982–1987) and Secretary of State George Shultz (1988).

A graduate of the University of Scranton (B.S., History, 1966), Dr. Sicherman earned his Ph.D. at the University of Pennsylvania (Political Science, 1971), where he received a Salvatori Fellowship. He is author or editor of numerous books and articles, including *America the Vulnerable: Our Military Problems and How to Fix Them* (FPRI, 2002) and *Palestinian Autonomy, Self-Government and Peace* (Westview Press, 1993). He edits *Peacefacts*, an FPRI bulletin that monitors the Arab-Israeli peace process.

MOHAMMAD PATEL is a freelance writer based in England. His interests include history and politics.